Computers In Broadcast and Cable Newsrooms

Using Technology in Television News Production

Computers In Broadcast and Cable Newsrooms

Using Technology in Television News Production

Phillip O. Keirstead, PhD
Florida A&M University

Routledge
Taylor & Francis Group
New York   London

First published by
Lawrence Erlbaum Associates,
10 Industrial Avenue
Mahwah, NJ 07430

Transferred to Digital Printing 2010

Routledge
Taylor & Francis Group
270 Madison Avenue
New York, NY 10016

Routledge
Taylor & Francis Group
2 Park Square
Milton Park, Abingdon
Oxon OX14 4RN

Cover design by Kathryn Houghtaling Lacey

Library of Congress Cataloging-in-Publication Data

Keirstead, Phillip O.
   Computers in broadcast and cable newsrooms : using technology in television news production / Phillip O. Keirstead.
     p. cm.
   Includes bibliographical references and index.
ISBN 0-8058-3063-4 (alk. Paper)
ISBN 0-8058-3064-2 (pbk. : alk. Paper)
    1. Television broadcasting of news—Production and direction. 2. Television broadcasting of news—Television innovations. I. Title.

PN4784.T4K387 2004
070.4'3—dc22
                                              2004046976
                                                   CIP

Contents

	Preface	vii
	Acknowledgments	ix
	Introduction	xiii
1	What Does a TV Producer Do?	1
2	The Heart of the Newsroom: What People Use to Produce the News and How They Do It	18
3	The Producer's Desk: Where it All Comes Together	29
4	Gathering Up the Bits and Pieces	50
5	The Production Team	69
6	The Assignment Desk	89
7	Computers in the Control Room	115
8	Computer-Assisted Reporting	130
9	Managing a Computerized Newsroom	143

10	Bells and Whistles	153
	Suggested Readings	166
	Index	167

Preface

Computers in Broadcast and Cable Newsrooms: Using Technology in Television News Production traces its origin to 1980, when the author began writing about television news technology in an effort to help television news managers cope with technological change.

Journalism is tied to technology. Although means of distributing news preceded the invention of the printing press, it was the technology of moveable type that allowed printers to reproduce copies of documents at reasonable cost, leading to the development of newspapers. Likewise, the invention of radio and television led to new and better ways to share information with large numbers of people.

Today's television news relies on varied and complex technologies to help journalists produce interesting, informative broadcasts. Television journalists must combine proficiency in fact-gathering, storytelling, and performance, while comfortably applying a variety of devices and technologies to publish their work. The complexity of creating a television news broadcast has created a need for a unique position—the producer. Producers are journalists who juggle the complex interpersonal management relationships inherent to a news staff, the editorial demands of accurate, ethical journalism, and the production devices and techniques that are employed to orchestrate a fast-moving, interesting, and informative news broadcast.

Acknowledgments

Assembling a textbook requires a team effort not unlike the creation of a news broadcast. The editor is the executive producer, the author is the producer, and the team is made up of an assortment of people, businesses, and institutions that contribute valuable elements to the final product. Our "executive producer" was Linda Bathgate of Lawrence Erlbaum Associates. Her team consisted of: Karin Wittig Bates and Marianna Vertullo.

The people who took on the challenge of creating computer systems specific to the needs of television news production deserve a tremendous ovation. Many were entrepreneurs who gambled their finances and their futures for an idea. Others were employees of technology and communication firms who stepped out of the safe and narrow to lead their companies in new directions. On the broadcast side, many people gambled on computer technology, devoting a tremendous amount of time to understanding this new technology because they had the foresight to see that computers were going to become essential to television newsgathering and production. There simply isn't sufficient space to list every name, and leaving anyone out would be a disservice. Many of the people who helped us acquire the knowledge that led to this book are mentioned in our history of newsroom computer system technology, *Automating Television News: A Generation of Change* (Castle Garden Press, 1999).

I am particularly grateful to two organizations that made it possible for me to study television news production in the very real environment of a television newsroom and a management seminar. I thank the John S. and James L. Knight Foundation and the Radio-Television News Directors Foundation for awarding us an Excellence in Journalism Education fellowship that allowed me to observe close up the workings of WMTW-TV News in Auburn and Portland, Maine. I also thank station manager and news director Dave Baer and his staff for their interest and patience in updating me on the techniques and challenges of producing TV news.

Thanks also go to the Poynter Institute in St. Petersburg, Florida for allowing us to participate in The Leadership Academy, a management seminar for midlevel news managers.

Many individuals in news organizations gave up valuable time to assist me in my research. They include Gina Gershon at Turner Broadcasting and Bruce Chong and Paul Reid at CNN News in Atlanta. Journalists at television stations who were extremely helpful include Juan Miguel Bassalik, director of news operations at WSVN-TV in Miami; WTVT Tampa general manger David Boylan, news director Phil Matlin, producer Allen Fetters, assignment editor John O'Laughlin, and director of engineering Cary Williams.

At KTNV in Las Vegas, I received valuable assistance from news director Perry Boxx and producer Ian Schank. Terry O'Reilly, who was senior vice president at the Weather Channel at the time, gave us a terrific tour of its Atlanta facilities. The Weather Channel is very dependent on producers to keep its rolling programming on track.

I also visited Channel One in London, a cable news channel that has since closed. During several stays in England, I toured the British Broadcasting Corporation (BBC), Independent Television News (ITN), and SkyNews, and their managers and news staffs have always been extremely cooperative. I should make special mention of Mel Martin, a veteran U.S. news executive who led a major project at the BBC Television News headquarters at White City that resulted in creation of the newsroom computer and automation system (ENPS) now offered by The Associated Press (AP). Dozens of AP people helped the author, but special thanks go to Lee Perryman, the overall head of ENPS and Eric Bowman, the European head of ENPS.

The news managers and staff of two stations in Tallahassee, Florida assisted me in many ways. Particular thanks go to station manager and news director Mike Smith of WCTV Television who gave me an opportunity to observe a news automation system in use and whose station has a decades-old tradition of being supportive of the broadcast faculty at Florida A&M University.

Doug Crary was news director at WTXL-TV in Tallahassee during a key phase of my research. Executive producer Dave Hansen and producer Jenny Laws were very helpful. WTXL, like its competitor, WCTV, has always been a good friend of journalism at Florida A&M. The management of Florida's News Channel, a cable news provider in Tallahassee also welcomed us into the newsroom. FNC was very helpful by demonstrating how virtual studio technology can benefit a television news organization. (Some of the people mentioned here have moved to other positions, but I list them in the context of research for this book.)

Tom Butts has been my editor at *TV Technology* magazine for several years and has helped me keep up with rapidly changing technology.

A faculty member who writes a book depends on an academic team that wants to see the project through. Florida A&M University demonstrated its confidence by granting me a one-semester sabbatical leave during which I worked on this and another book. Thanks go to the school's instructor/librarian, Gloria Woody, for her

ACKNOWLEDGMENTS

support. Students and graduates also provided me with information and ideas as to what this book should contain.

Most of all, my deepest gratitude goes to my co-author on other projects and chief editor and idea person, S-K. Keirstead, who has suffered through eight other books, providing skilled editorial advice and motivation (whatever it took) to get on with the task.

—Phillip O. Keirstead
Wiscasset, Maine
June, 2003

Introduction

This book describes the New World of Journalism:

Producers and computers ...

Assignment editors and computers ...

Reporters and computers ...

Writers and computers ...

The text and pictures gathered by a television news team are computer assembled into a package called a newscast, magazine show, documentary, news event, or news bulletin. The Newsroom Computer System is the backbone of the automation system that supports a news broadcast. The system stores all the video, audio, writing, and graphics that make up a broadcast until needed.

People determine the content and style of the broadcast. *Computers* help to keep the team organized, improve production, and provide new methods to reuse the product. Some newsroom computer systems function as automation guidance systems, which direct the devices needed to produce a news or special events broadcast.

Producers use computer systems as a tool to create their product. We will be looking at how producers who orchestrate the presentation of news broadcasts use these systems.

Many people do not understand the role of the producer of a news broadcast. Producers are responsible for determining *what* goes on the air, *when* it goes on the air, *how* it goes on the air, and *who* will present the news story. The producer develops a strategy for covering the day's news for a specific broadcast, and then guides the development of each item in the news broadcast, by directing editors, reporters, technicians, and news sources. The producer reduces the logistics of assembling all of the parts of news program to a *rundown,* a paper and electronic roadmap that is used to put the program on the air. The producer works with a director while the live news program is on the air, modifying the content, and controlling the timing to assure that the broadcast concludes on time.

A news broadcast will only be as good as the producer who guides it through the creative process. Producers determine the style and length of each story. They weave an "inventory" of stories into a cohesive rundown that represents the order and content of the day's news stories. Producers solve logistics problems, assign reporters and videographers, run down facts to insert in new stories, write scripts, and approve scripts written by others.

The reason that computer technology is a major focus of this textbook is that computer systems are the universal tools that tie television news together. Every television newsroom in the U.S. (and most of the rest of the world) relies on computer technology to prepare and broadcast news.

If you say "wow" at the end of news broadcast—credit the team that created the parts—but focus on the producer who brought it all together and the director who executed the plan.

A SMALL ASSUMPTION

People in the communication field must be able to use a personal computer. So, we assume you can turn on a personal computer (PC) and can type a news story.

FIG. I.1. Some producers work for international newsgathering agencies, securing and editing video feeds for use by network and station clients. Image courtesy of Associated Press Television News.

INTRODUCTION   xv

- You should learn how to use a computer equipped with Microsoft® Windows® software.
- You should learn how to use "windows" programs, that is, how to move from one window to another, for example, between a story you are writing, and something in a file, or between your writing screen and the Internet. If you become familiar with Microsoft® Windows®, your learning curve will be much faster when you encounter an actual newsroom system.
- The majority of computers used in broadcast newsroom systems are in the DOS/Windows operating system family—they are not Apple products, and although you can learn some very basic computer skills on a MAC computer by Apple, these are not the computers you are likely to be using.
- You should visit TV newsrooms (you ought to be doing this anyway). Get to know some people, especially people who work nights and weekends. Be an intern, work in the "real world" and you are almost guaranteed you will at least be taught the basics of the newsroom computer system.

COMPUTER 101

What is a broadcast newsroom computer system?

It starts with a *desktop personal computer* or if you're really fortunate, a sophisticated *desktop workstation*. Workstations are high-priced computer terminals that create graphics, play audio, and show video. Typically the desktop configuration will consist of a monitor, a keyboard, a mouse, speakers, and a "central processing unit" (CPU).

The computers journalists use emphasize word-processing. In a newsroom, the desktop computers are usually connected by some type of network made up of cables and software. If the network is large, one or more computers may be assigned just to running the network. These are called *servers* because they store and serve up stories, wire copy, and other materials when we need them. The first big step in developing newsroom systems was connecting press agency wires to the computer. Newsrooms need to be able to read and sort the fast, constant flow of news copy that they are receiving. By connecting the press wire to the computer, we avoid the inconvenience and cost of having to print out wire copy that is coming to us at 1,200 words per minute. Instead, we go to the index page in our computer program and read the brief descriptions of the latest news stories. When we find a story we want to read, we click the *mouse* on a title or symbol (icon) that makes the computer bring up the story on the monitor screen. If we need a paper copy, we give the computer a command and it instructs the printer to print it.

The press agencies have worked very closely with the newsroom computer industry and the Radio-Television News Directors Association (RTNDA) to devise codes that tell computers how to sort incoming stories by category for the brief listings. This eliminates paper and gives everyone who is authorized an opportunity to access wire copy at their desk.

Having a network allows the newsroom staff to send information, messages, pictures, video, audio, and stories to each other. Television news is based on teamwork, and careful double-checking, so it is important to be able to access stories others have written or produced.

A writer composes a news script on the computer and sends it electronically to an editor or producer. The assignment desk leaves a message for the nighttime producer in an e-mail or that person's computer notepad. A reporter brings up last month's city council script from the archives. A video editor retrieves pictures of the warehouse fire last month. The news director takes a look at the preliminary rundown for the 6 p.m. news on her desktop computer. These are typical activities that are going on at the same time on the newsroom network, all tied together by the ubiquitous computer.

A newsroom computer system can be built so that we can insert instructions or *cues* in our scripts that direct various devices to activate when they are needed during the broadcast. This is *automation*.

OUR JOURNEY BEGINS

By the time you have read this book and completed the course associated with it, you should have a basic working knowledge about producing the news using the computer technology in television newsrooms. There is a tremendous demand for television news producers. Every television news broadcast needs to have at least one person who brings all the elements together into an informative and interesting program.

Producing television news is like coaching a team. A producer works within a framework for a specific program. The framework is called a *format*. It defines the opening and closing, the number of commercial breaks, the amount of time for content, and the overall length. In television news a format usually indicates the type of content that will be put in certain segments, which is why the weather forecast always appears at about the same place in a specific news broadcast.

A coach works within a framework, which is defined by the nature of the sport, its level—high school or college—and some external rules, such as those of the National Collegiate Athletic Association (NCAA).

A producer works with a team: associate producers, production assistants, an assignment editor, reporters, videographers, video editors, audio engineers, and operations producers. The producer decides the strategy and coordinates who does what. The producer evaluates the stories that are developed and determines their style (voice/over, voice/over-sound on tape, or a full package), length, and position in the broadcast.

The producer coaches, encouraging the reporters and videographers to seek more information and shoot original video. Associate producers are sent scrambling for supporting information whereas production assistants are looking in the archives for file video.

Finally, all the effort comes together for the game—the news program, which is broadcast directly from the producer's rundown, a professional description of every

FIG. I.2. Digital technology makes it possible for correspondents in remote locations to send text, audio, and video over compact portable satellite transmission devices, including satellite telephones. Image courtesy of Livewire, U.K.

production move that needs to take place to put the broadcast on the air the way the public will see and listen to it. A *rundown* is a game plan.

Producers are important, it takes a special sort of skill and talent to take the players you're given and coax them into a giving a winning performance. And just as in coaching, there's no rehearsal, when the whistle blows, the game (broadcast) begins!

1
What Does a TV Producer Do?

Explaining what a television news producer does can be difficult because most of what a producer does is hidden from public view. All we see when we watch news on TV are the anchors, reporters, weather presenters, and sportscasters. The measure of a well-produced program is that how it gets on the air should not be seen or heard by the audience. A well-produced news program should be "seamless," meaning that nothing distracts or detracts from the information being presented.

Why are producers such a big deal in television news? The "big deal" is that the producer is in charge of the program. What goes into it, how much exposure a reporter gets on air, and the length of the weather segment are all decided by the producer. Anchorpeople and reporters are the public aspect of a news program, but the anchors and reporters do what the producer tells them to do!

Ask a news director who has the most important job in the newsroom? She or he will tell you, the producer. What's the most difficult position to fill in a newsroom? Producer. Why? Because we all get our initial exposure to broadcast news on television (or cable) from people we come to recognize as anchors, reporters, weather presenters, and sportscasters. These are the "glamour" jobs. Naturally, when we are learning about broadcast journalism, we want to imitate the television "stars." Producers work very hard and deal with a lot of pressure. The producer has authority over the on-air personalities, but the producer gets little public recognition when a program is outstanding. Why do some people choose to be producers?

Frequently it's because their egos don't strive for public recognition, they get their satisfaction from pulling together the widely scattered parts of a program, and making the product look as if it just happened naturally. It's the same sort of drive that motivates movie producers, theater directors, or corporate managers. The desire to be the controlling force that makes things happen.

ON THE FIRING LINE

Another way to understand what producers do is to become an unseen observer. We describe a real television newsroom ... in a television market somewhere between 75 and 100. (The size of markets is determined by a combination of government statistical areas (SMSAs—Standard Metropolitan Statistical Areas) and the actual clustering of television stations. The industry-accepted list of markets is published annually by Nielsen Media Research, a television rating service. Examples of television markets in the 75 to 100 group would include: Spokane, Washington; Columbia, South Carolina; Madison, Wisconsin; and Burlington, Vermont-Plattsburg, New York.

The station is an ABC Television affiliate. Karen, the assignment editor, arrives at work just before 7 a.m., ahead of the producers. She logs in on her terminal and scans the list of possible assignments, mainly to see what the nightside staff has added since yesterday. Then she looks quickly at the rundown for the 11 p.m. news, to see if any spot or breaking news stories ran at 11 p.m. that were not in the 5:00 p.m., 5:30 p.m., and 6:00 p.m. newscasts last night.

Karen doesn't have to wade through a file folder full of future stories and story ideas because they are entered into the computer when they arrive at the assignment desk. Paper files are kept as backups.

If there is an early morning story in the assignment file, a reporter and/or videographer should already have the assignment. However, if Karen feels that a scheduled event needs coverage before the 9 a.m. morning meeting, she either dispatches the early shift videographer, or she calls staff members at home and dispatches them to cover the assignment. Some mornings a crew will already be working when Karen arrives, usually because a spot news story has broken overnight or in the early morning hours.

Next, it's time for a cup of coffee, and a quick read through four daily newspapers, to see if the papers have turned up stories Karen doesn't know about. In some cases, the papers become the source for information about upcoming events, especially in fringe areas within the station's coverage pattern. (For purposes of our discussion, a VHF station [channels 2–13] may radiate an acceptable signal as much as 100 miles from its tower, but typically the area covered by the news department will be smaller, depending on the distribution of cities and towns within the market.) On Thursday, Karen also scans (on-line) eight area weekly papers, looking for interesting news stories and feature ideas.

While Karen is moving through the morning routine, she keeps an ear tuned to the three public safety scanners in the background, listening for reports of severe accidents, fires, or other emergencies. She only keeps one ear tuned to the scanners because the other one is listening to telephone calls. Karen makes a quick, routine sweep of police agencies and fire departments, seeking spot news. Usually she speaks to a dispatcher or to the shift commander. She also receives a dozen incoming calls from the news director, producers, reporters, and videographers checking in. The radio news director also calls, comparing assignments for the day and swapping tips.

WHAT DOES A TV PRODUCER DO?

FIG. 1.1. TV news anchors must cope with technology such as these computer-driven prompters mounted on the studio cameras. Image courtesy of BDLAutoscript Ltd.

Thanks to computer technology, Karen also does a quick check of key Web sites, looking for story ideas. The time does fly when you're busy, and pretty soon it's 9 a.m. and time for the morning meeting. Karen's job is to set up the list of known story possibilities for the day, and make some early decisions on who will cover what stories. Later, we spend more time with an assignment editor, and learn how a newsroom computer system helps the assignment desk through its chaotic day.

THE MORNING MEETING

A beginning of the day—Morning Meeting—occurs in every television newsroom around the country. In some instances, a telephone "conference call" is held earlier, to facilitate decisions, and cope with commuting problems in larger cities. In addition, key players in the assignment process usually access the newsroom computer system from home to look through the rundowns from the previous evening's late news and look at the list of potential assignments for this day.

Many news directors prefer to let the lead producer, usually called the *executive producer*, chair the morning meeting. This creates a more collegial atmosphere that encourages contributions by everyone attending the meeting. In stations with smaller staffs, it is not unusual for all staff members who are in the newsroom at the time to attend the morning meeting and suggest stories. In larger news organizations, reporters, videographers, editors, and technicians may be represented by producers or supervisors. On the technical side, larger news organizations usually have an *operations manager* who speaks for the technical staff, which may include live truck operators, videographers, editors, and technical assistants.

CHANNEL 10, OUR EXAMPLE

The custom at Channel 10 is for the assignment editor to discuss pending and potential assignments, while Bob, the executive producer, chairs the meeting, asking questions and making decisions regarding what stories will be covered and how. The core staff is small. Bob also produces the 6 p.m. news. Tamika, who sits opposite Bob, produces the 5:00 and 5:30 p.m. broadcasts. She and Bob discuss assignments and allocation of resources as the meeting progresses. The news director, Jorgé, stands off to the side, surveying the assignment board and listening. Pearl, the operations producer, sits at a nearby workstation. She is responsible for assigning video editors and operations production assistants, as well as developing graphics for the broadcasts. Pearl's workstation is specially designed to manipulate images into the graphics that are seen behind the anchors or within individual news stories. She gets a great deal of her raw material from images available on the Internet. She also pulls scenes from tapes shot by the videographers, and the station's archives.

Karen runs down the list of assigned and potential stories on a wall chart. Some routine items will already have staff members assigned. For example, one anchorperson is also the health reporter. She is ready to do her health package today, so Karen assigns a videographer to shoot and edit the package. They will start early because the anchor has to be back in the newsroom by mid-afternoon to prepare for her broadcasts.

There are also *franchises*, informational features that are supplied by outside syndicators, but require narration by local talent. The morning cut-in anchor, Celia, is going to narrate her feature as soon as the meeting is over. An editor will work with her to wrap up the piece for tonight's 5 p.m. news block.

The early videographer, Carl, comes in from the scene of an early morning house fire. He gives everyone a quick synopsis of what took place, and suggests he and a reporter go out later in the morning to interview the director of municipal utilities to determine if work on a nearby gas main had anything to do with the fire. Bob asks Celia to do a telephone check and see if the gas line construction work is being investigated as a possible cause of the fire.

Karen then runs down the list of possible assignments, which include:

- A news conference to announce the receipt of a federal education grant for the Pinewood School District.
- The former mayor of Topsville was arrested last night, after he got into a fistfight with another motorist in the parking lot of the Northwoods Shopping Center. The former mayor was arrested and booked by police, but released later on his own recognizance.

WHAT DOES A TV PRODUCER DO?

- The local United Fund Drive will be kicked off during a noon luncheon at the Civic Center.
- State Senator Cynthia Legalis is making a multistop sweep of the second congressional district to announce that she is "feeling the pulse of the public" before she decides whether or not to run for congress.
- Paul, the morning weather anchor, says the heat wave of the past week is not going to break today—in fact, local high temperature records may be set.
- Samson Township police have arrested a 22-year-old man who they believe was involved in a hit and run automobile fatality. The suspect was supposed to be home, under house detention and wearing a corrections department ankle alarm. Two years ago he was convicted as an accomplice in the murder of an elderly farmer.
- The assignment desk got an e-mail this morning from a homeowner on Paige Street. It seems the homeowner has put up basketball backboards on an unused city right-of-way adjacent to his home. The homeowner said for the past 6 years he has voluntarily coached neighborhood youth, who scrimmage on his ad hoc basketball court. Now, three neighbors are complaining about the noise and are threatening to petition the City Council, seeking to force the homeowner to stop using the abandoned dead-end street. The homeowner claims he is keeping local teens out of trouble by providing the basketball court. He also points out the lack of city recreation facilities in his area.
- A conservation group contacted the news director late yesterday, asking for coverage of its protest in front of the State Capitol this afternoon. The group opposed construction of a flood-control dam on the Scargo River. The state capital is 35 miles from the Channel 10 studios.
- Paula, the features reporter, needs a videographer for the day. She plans to go to Bassick Falls to do a human interest story about a woman who builds harpsichords.
- The Falsoe County Grand Jury is expected to hand up indictments in three major criminal cases sometime this afternoon.
- In Scargo County, the first degree murder trial of a man accused to killing two fast food restaurant workers during a holdup is expected to go to the jury.

That's the preliminary line-up at 9 o'clock in the morning.

DECISION MAKING

Now we have a list of potential stories. Let's see what happens to them:

- Bob tells Celia, the morning anchor, to do her feature narration and then go with Carl to do a followup on the house fire. Although Carl and Celia started work early, they will stay with the story until they are confident they have as much information as they can get today. Celia may end up having to do a live report during the early evening new block. If a gas main fault continues to be suspected, this could be a major story tonight. Luckily for Carl and Celia, Channel 10 does not do a noon news broadcast, or they would have to prepare a story by 11:30 a.m. or so, depending on whether it was live or on tape.

- Pinewood Grant: The federal grant of $980,000 is a big item for the Pinewood School District, but the station can't spare a reporter, so a videographer will go to the event. She will set up the camera to record the presentation ceremony, then interview the Superintendent of Schools (from behind the camera), and finish up by shooting some video of the Middle School and a science laboratory that will benefit from grant funds. She will have to get permission from the school's principal and the classroom teacher before shooting the activity video in the science lab. Different education jurisdictions have their own rules about videography or photography in classrooms when students are present. The general video will be used as *voice-over* or VO, in which an anchor reads the script while pictures of the school and the science lab are shown on the screen. This video is also useful when editing in the sound-on-tape (SOT) interviews or presentations.

- Former Topsville mayor arrested: Bob, the executive producer, says this is a tough call, after all, it's the *former* mayor. He doesn't think he will have room for more than a brief mention in the 6 p.m. half hour. Tamika says she could use a brief piece because she has to fill two half hours, the 5:00 and 5:30 p.m. broadcasts. They ask Karen if she can talk Paula into stopping in Topsville for a few minutes on the way to her feature. Karen has already called the former mayor, who says he doesn't have any comment. The politician's attorney has also declined to be interviewed. The Topsville police chief says he is available to do a short, facts-only interview. Other than that, the only video is likely to be some general scenes of the shopping center. Karen calls Paula, who agrees to do the story. Paula will also attempt to find the motorist who was involved in the reported altercation.

- United Fund: A routine, but important, story because many segments of the local community will be collecting funds. Karen says she has already assigned a reporter and videographer who are to prepare a voice-over story for the 5:00 or 5:30 p.m., and a longer piece with sound-on-tape (SOT) for the 6 p.m. Bob and Tamika will decide how to position the story versions later in the day. Pearl says she will pull some charts off the United Fund Web site, in case they are needed. Bob says: "Don't forget their logo (trademark), we'll probably need it for the Chromakey (the picture over the anchor's shoulder)."

- Senator Legalis: There are only two congressional districts in the state, and Channel 10 covers all of the First District and part of the Second, so this political story is important, even though the candidate has not officially announced that she is running. She will be in town at 2 this afternoon. It's decided to send the crew from the United Fund event to her campaign stop. Tamika reminds Pearl

that she should retrieve the state map graphics that show the two congressional districts to help people visualize the area the congressperson serves.
- Heat: Jorgé, the news director, says: "Let's make this a team effort. Have all crews look for 'heat' related video, such as bank signs; melting asphalt; hot, sweaty workers; ice cream trucks; and wherever possible, crews should try to grab brief interviews to drop in as sound-on-tape bits." He suggests that the evening meteorologist, Dr. Susan Chao, do a special live wrap-around for the 6 p.m. broadcast. Tamika asks if she could plan a shorter version for the 5 p.m. broadcast, and Jorgé agrees to her idea. Jorgé is constantly reminding producers that weather is one story that is universal to all viewers.
- Samson Township arrest: Karen says this involves travel, and no one is currently slated to be in the Samson Township area. However, she has contacted the Sheriff's office, and they are e-mailing her the booking mug shot of the suspect. Everyone agrees, this one is a *reader*, meaning it will be read by one of the anchors. Calls will be made later in the day to update the story.
- Bob says he likes the Paige Street basketball story. Karen says she thinks Channel 10 has it exclusively because the homeowner addressed his e-mail to her personally, and she remembers meeting him at a civic event last fall. Bob says "This one deserves its own crew, and maybe the live truck if it develops into a good story." Everyone agrees, and Karen assigns a reporter and videographer. She notifies engineering that she may need the microwave truck (a custom-built vehicle equipped with a transmitter that relays sound and pictures back to the station) at the Paige Street site this afternoon.
- Tamika says she would like the state capital conservation protest story, but Karen says she thinks the satellite truck will be needed elsewhere. Right now, Karen doesn't have a crew she can spare for a story that involves a 70 mile round trip.
- Falsoe County Grand Jury. Karen says the current plan is to have the crew from the candidate event at 2 p.m. go to the courthouse. She adds that grand juries don't usually work late, so there should be some report in time for the news block. Grand Jury sessions are closed, so a production assistant will be assigned to pull file video relevant to the cases, Paula will check for mug shots, and the reporter will probably do a standup outside the courthouse. The District Attorney, who conducts the Grand Jury session, usually will not make herself available following a Grand Jury session.

Jorgé comments that this does not make a particularly visual television story, but he wants the station to be more proactive in following major crime cases from their occurrence, through the investigation, and then covering the major steps leading up the trial coverage. Cameras are permitted in trial courtrooms under rules set down by the State Supreme Court.
- The discussion then turns to the first-degree murder trial in Scargo County. At this point, Karen either has to commit her last reporter or arrange for one of the anchors to break away to cover the jury deliberations. Bob says: "This case is so sensational, and there has been so much interest in it, we need to push the en-

velope. Let's send Carol Ogara [the 5:30 p.m. co-anchor] and the night videographer. Call Pete (the videographer) and say we need him in early. They'll just have to stake out the courthouse. Jason Williams is going to have to do the 5:30 show by himself." Bob tells Pearl she should prepare a "bulletin" visual, in case a decision is announced while the news is live. Tamika says she will have a production assistant locate and edit some file tape to use with the reporter's standup in front of the courthouse. Information about the V/O tape will be sent by wireless connection to the reporter's laptop computer.

Karen says: "Do we send the satellite truck?"

Bob replies: "Yes, it's a gamble, but it's one we've got to take. If the jury comes in late this afternoon, it's the only way we're going to get the story into the early block."

Karen calls engineering and gives them the order for the satellite truck. The engineering supervisor says the truck is in the garage for minor servicing, but it should be ready by 10 a.m.

Jorgé takes a couple of minutes to discuss some long term projects, and to remind everyone that he wants more original stories that result from the staff's ideas and contacts.

WHAT HAPPENS NEXT?

Bob and Tamika spend a couple of minutes going over their notes, deciding how they think they will divide up today's inventory of stories over three 30-minute early-evening broadcasts. Then they both turn to their computer terminals. Tamika immediately begins typing story names and approximate times into the rundowns for each of her programs. The framework or *format* for each broadcast, which is the opening, the breaks for commercials, and the closing, as well as descriptions of segment content, such as weather or sports, are permanently listed on each rundown screen. Tamika types in the information that changes, including story names, production information, and times.

Bob usually holds off outlining his rundown until he updates himself by reading the wire service news briefs on his terminal screen. While they are working on organizing the broadcasts, Karen is on the phone, giving instructions to the crews.

The rest of the morning is spent researching the assigned stories, reading incoming wire stories, and checking other sources for possible assignments. Bob and Karen have production assistants backing them up, whereas Tamika is joined later by an associate producer, who helps her with juggling the back-to-back half-hour news programs. The night producer comes in after lunch, in time for the afternoon meeting. She can and often does help the early evening producers when the newsroom gets busy.

As soon as Bob has typed in his preliminary rundown, he puts aside his "producer" role, and becomes a manager, working on the staff schedule for upcoming weeks. Bob is responsible for scheduling assignment editors, producers, associate producers, assistant producers, and newsroom production assistants. The chief

WHAT DOES A TV PRODUCER DO?

videographer sets up the shift schedule for the videographers. Pearl works out the schedule for the tape editors who are not videographers.

Pearl makes a quick list of editing assignments she will have to give out, and then goes to work surfing the Web for visuals she can used to create graphics.

The newsroom takes on the late morning hum, punctuated by mouse clicks as people work on their computers, telephones buzz, and the public safety monitors are droning.

"Washaw County to Ridgeton Fire."

"Ridgeton, go ahead."

"Ridgeton, a Mrs. Davis at 27-32 Parmel Highway reports the ceiling has collapsed on the second floor of her house, it is unclear whether or not she is trapped." (Karen spins around and punches up "56" on another public safety monitor. This is the Ridgeton Fire/Rescue and police channel. This way she locks the monitor on the Ridgeton transmissions. Washaw County is the emergency 911 dispatch center for the area.)

"Ridgeton Dispatch: Rescue One, Patrol 103, occupant, a Mrs. Davis, at 27-32 Parmel Highway, reports ceiling collapsed, she may be trapped."

"Rescue One, acknowledged."

"103, 10-4."

"Washaw Sheriff Unit Four."

"Go ahead Four."

FIG. 1.2. This satellite-dish equipped Humvee provides a means to transmit television news stories from remote areas. Image courtesy of Associated Press Television News.

"We're 3 minutes from the Parmel Highway address."
"Thank you Four, please assist Rescue One, Patrol 103."
"10-4".

By now, Karen is on the phone, trying to reach Paula who is on her way to Topsville. Karen tells her to go to the Ridgeton address, just in case the incident turns into a story.

A half-hour later Paula calls, only a portion of the ceiling in one room came down because the elderly lady had stored too many magazines in the attic. Local volunteers are going to fix the ceiling and clean out the attic. Paula and the videographer continue on to Topsville.

Bob eats lunch at his desk, a production assistant calls for lunch delivery for several people in the newsroom. Sometimes staff members go out for lunch, but someone has to stay behind to cover the phones. Every staff member's telephone number, cellphone number and pager number is entered in the staff directory section of the computer system, in case they need to be located.

Manny, the radio news director, calls. He got a tip that a big commercial Web site with offices in a nearby business park is going to lay off 100 of its employees. Karen checks with Bob, then arranges for the second night videographer to meet a reporter at the company's offices. Manny was told the company will notify its employees at about 4 p.m.. The crew will try to get an interview with a company official and a couple of laid-off employees. In the meantime a desk assistant will look up background information on the firm in the newsroom computer archives and online (by checking area newspaper sites for business articles on the company).

Bob tells Tamika about the story. She decides to lead the 5 p.m. broadcast with a brief story. Bob plans to use a full reporter package. He tentatively assigns the layoff story the lead spot in his broadcast because, although the number of people to be laid-off is small, the story ties in to the larger issue of the local economy and the general health of the "dot com" industry. Bob then begins to scan his notes and the wires for other business stories that might be positioned next to the layoff package in the first section of the 6 p.m. broadcast.

AFTERNOON MEETING

Just after 2 p.m. another meeting is held. Karen, Bob, Tamika, Pearl, and the night producer, Melanie, talk over the day's news flow from their desks. Jorgé doesn't attend today because he is in a budget meeting with the station's general manager.

Karen quickly reviews the assignment list:

- The new lay-off story is now the priority effort.
- City officials won't confirm that a gas line problem might have been the cause of the early morning house fire, but Celia talked to a state fire marshal, who said he was not ruling out a gas explosion because the home shows signs of an explosion taking place and there is no other indication of a cause of the fire. Bob decides to go with a package, unless additional information regarding a pos-

WHAT DOES A TV PRODUCER DO?

sible gas line problem becomes available. He assigns an intern to do a computer search to see if there have been any other gas line problems involving the local utility or its supplier. Celia and Carl shot scenes of the fire site and talked with the fire chief, the state fire marshal, and the homeowners. Celia will write two standups and then they will return to the station to finish writing and editing two packages and two voice-overs to cover the 5, 5:30, 6 and 11 p.m. broadcasts. They also shot a little tape of firefighters "mopping up" the fire scene in the intense late morning heat, in case it is needed for the heat wave story.

- Paula did interview the Topsville police chief and they shot location video. Tamika asks for a short package for the 5:30 p.m., and a voice-over for the 5 p.m. Bob says he wants a voice-over with sound-on-tape (VO/SOT) to be read by the 6 p.m. anchor.

- The Pinewood grant story went as planned. The videographer will cut a VO/SOT for the 5 p.m. and VO tapes for the 5:30 and 6 p.m.. The 11 p.m. producer asks Karen to find out if there is enough tape available for her to have a different VO piece for the 11 p.m.

- The United Fund story will go as planned. Bob says that he may not have room for a package on the 6 p.m., so he and Tamika swap packages. She will take the package and Bob will use the brief item.

- The United Fund crew got to the Senator Legalis story. It turned out to be an interesting assignment. The senator was meeting at a local restaurant with a group of supporters, some of whom had attended the local high school with her. The videographer set up microphones so that he could record both the senator and some of the people at the table. Mainly he recorded the senator talking, but he broke away three times to tape one of the supporters asking a question, so he would have cutaway shots to cover any edits. The style of the story is to let the participants tell the story. The reporter did two short introductions outside the restaurant, in case they are needed. Bob indicated he might let the anchors narrate and then run excerpts from the "conversation" in the restaurant.

While the crew was there, they did a separate interview with the restaurant owner about customers' lunch preferences when the temperature soars into the high 90s. The owner said people switch from their standard fare of hot sandwiches and fries to iced tea and salads. The interview will be given to the associate producer who is preparing the "heat wave story." The other crews will bring in tape to add to the story, which may be handled live as a news story by the weather presenter.

- The Paige Street basketball story could develop into a major local controversy. The reporter has determined that no other media have been contacted and he has gotten interviews with the homeowner, some of the neighborhood teens and two nearby homeowners who don't like the ad hoc basketball games. He also talked to the head of the city planning department regarding zoning and land-use issues. Bob decides to use the live truck and give the story the lead position in the second section of the 6 p.m. broadcast. He urges Tamika to position a live shot near the top of the 5 p.m., and again, further down in the 5:30 p.m. rundown. The 11 p.m. producer asks for a package for her broadcast. She says she will check and see of the early stories cause enough controversy, and if so, she would assign a night reporter to do a followup. Otherwise, Bob plans a followup story tomorrow.

- The two courthouse stories are still pending. Bob and Tamika have written several readers that can be used by the anchors, who will also write additional short items, based on telephone reporting and wire service stories.

The meeting breaks up. Karen's desk assistant does another telephone sweep of the police and fire agencies while Karen inputs the interesting future items that arrived by e-mail and regular mail into the assignment log. She also does a briefing e-mail for the night producer.

The night assignment desk is covered by an associate assignment editor, who is similar to an associate producer. Jorgé would like to have a more experienced person in the slot, but his budget is too tight. Fortunately, he was able to hire a former 911 dispatcher who took early retirement, and who Jorgé hopes to develop into a full-fledged assignment editor when the budget allows.

THE TEMPO INCREASES

By 2:30 in the afternoon you can detect a subtle change in the newsroom. The phone is ringing more frequently, videographers and reporters are beginning to come in from their assignments, production assistants are rushing about, checking the wires, locating file videotape, running internet checks for background. Tape editors are calling to confirm editing instructions while Pearl is busy at her terminal, searching the Internet for visual material she can give to the graphic artists, who are responsible for creating the visuals that accompany stories, either as part of the story or as *keys* (taken from Chromakey, a method of inserting pictures over the shoulders, or behind the anchors.)

One production assistant is responsible for monitoring all of the incoming *feeds*. These are closed-circuit satellite transmissions of features, stories, and raw video that are supplied by the network and independent vendors, such as CNN and APTN. Much of the network material comes from the station cooperative, a network-managed unit that collects stories from affiliates and then sends selected items out as prearranged feeds. The producers draw from these resources to make their broadcasts more visual. Typically producers look for interesting features, raw video of regional, national or international stories, and regional items outside the station's primary coverage area.

The network, and other vendors, provide live feeds of major news stories. These are fed at set times, so that the live feed can be used close to the top of a local station's broadcast. Bob has a local breaking story planned at the top of his 6 p.m. broadcast, so he will have tonight's live report on the World Economic Summit taped for replay later in the broadcast.

Scripts, rundowns and some video feeds are accessed through the Internet. Most producers scan the rundowns, and then ask a production assistant to copy the stories for viewing, and possible use. Some newsroom computer systems have a browse function that permits a producer to call up any news story as a file and view it in *low-resolution* (poorer, but viewable quality) on their workstation screen. The stories are stored in digital computer servers that are accessed through a computer network linked to each newsroom terminal.

At Channel 10 the assignment desk is also responsible for updating the station's Web site. Usually Karen's production assistant writes brief items as soon as story scripts are finished by reporters, anchors, or producers. The assignment desk also updates information promoting the major stories that will be covered on the upcoming news broadcasts. The station has a Webmaster who works out of the radio newsroom, but tight staffing requires help from the TV and radio newsrooms in order to keep the Web site up-to-date. The radio side is providing streaming audio to the Web and TV streams its news broadcasts. Next year Channel 10 plans to install software that will allow producers to send selected video stories to the Web.

CRUNCH TIME

Tamika has finished the rundowns for her 5 p.m. and 5:30 p.m. broadcasts. She has the voice-overs, readers, and feed stories written and inserted into her rundown, which is a sophisticated list of everything that is used or will occur during the broadcast (more about this later). Her screen has a series of check-off points and color codes that tell Tamika and her assistants what items are complete and checked for air. The same system indicates the status of each story that has been inserted into the rundown. Each position on the rundown has been filled in, although this does not indicate the two broadcasts are locked-up. Tamika will make changes during the next 2 hours, and if she has to, she can insert a new story or move stories around up to about 1 minute before they are due to go on the air.

While Tamika works on scripts, Lin is writing the copy for the *bumpers,* the promotional voice-overs that end each segment and promote the content of the next segment. Once Tamika approves the scripts, Lin will make a list of video to be copied to provide pictures to cover the text.

The public safety monitor (scanner) comes to life:

"303" (303 is a state police patrol unit number)

"303"

"303, report of tanker overturned at milepost 67. Scargo County Fire/Rescue and Baypoint Fire notified and en route."

"10-4"

Karen's assistant runs over to the public safety monitor, turns up the volume and locks it on the state police channel. Karen is already speed dialing a night videographer's cellphone. "Robert ... the state has an overturned tanker at milepost 67, northbound side on I-43. You head over there, I'll tell your supervisor to shuffle the editing schedule. Thanks." Bob and Tamika are both listening, realizing an accident involving a tanker truck on the interstate could affect rush hour traffic. Bob says: "Karen, pull the satellite truck off the Scargo Courthouse story and send it, the crew and Carol Ogara over to the Interstate. Then get a videographer and a reporter over to the Courthouse so we can at least get video for the 11 p.m. if the jury verdict comes in."

The phones are really busy now, as assignments are shuffled, to free up videographers and still get the editing done for the early block. An intern is detailed to relay the story to radio news and the Webmaster.

"303 to dispatch."

"Go ahead."

"We have a chemical tanker off the road. It crossed the median from the southbound lane and is partially blocking the northbound outside. The tank is leaking an unknown fluid. The tractor is leaking fuel. Rescue is trying to extract the driver. A fire crew is spraying foam on the tank. We have four other vehicles involved with injuries. A Scargo sheriff's unit has the southbound side stopped, we are blocking northbound. All traffic in both directions is stopped. We need hazmat, EPA, ambulances and assistance."

"10-4 303."

"300"

"300, go ahead"

"300 ... 303 has a major traffic accident with injuries, hazardous materials spill at I-43, milepost 67. Fire/rescue and sheriff on scene. Assistance being dispatched."

"10-4, have 303 meet me on tach 2" (300 is the state police district commander, who wants the patrol officer to speak to him on a secure, scrambled frequency). While the dispatcher was notifying the district commander, another dispatcher was sending additional state police and sheriff's units, ambulances, a hazardous material unit, and a state environmental disaster team. Once the emergency units are dispatched, the control center calls the state police public information officer at district headquarters. She will call the media instead of waiting for their calls because the public needs to be warned about the road blockage, which will require detouring rush hour traffic.

Bob is on the phone talking to Jorgé, the news director. Jorgé authorizes Bob to call in an off-duty videographer and reporter. The severity of the situation and the difficulty of moving around the scene will probably require two crews. If they can get their video back to the satellite truck, Channel 10 will be able to get video on the early news to emphasize to people how serious the situation is. Tamika tells Bob the truck operator called and said he was able to get his truck within camera range of the wreck. He has set up a live camera on a tripod on top of the truck and is transmitting live video.

Bob calls the news promotion coordinator, who is responsible for producing live and recorded news promotions and tells her she has live video available for the 4 p.m. news update. Karen, who has stayed beyond her shift, has alerted the four anchors to be ready to do instant updates, as well as live promotion spots. The night assignment editor has alerted engineering and the staff director that a major story has broken.

FIG. 1.3. How"s this for an office? Today"s correspondents can write stories, edit video, and transmit their material using a laptop computer and a digital satellite uplink or satellite telephone, while sitting in the shade of an armored vehicle. Image courtesy of Associated Press Television News.

Two assistant producers and an intern are making phone calls, trying to get information on traffic rerouting and more specifics on casualties.

Tamika is frantically working to rearrange the 5 p.m. broadcast, while Bob has called up her 5:30 p.m. rundown on his screen, and he is reorganizing the rundown. Pearl has already retrieved maps from the Internet, and she has a series of graphics ready, including one for the upcoming promotion cut-in.

The phone rings at the assignment desk. It's the reporter from the Scargo County Courthouse. The jury has sent the judge a note indicating it has reached a decision. Court bailiffs are rounding up the defense and prosecution teams. Karen tells the reporter to get as much video as possible. Karen tells the reporter to do a quick opening and close and then rush the video to the satellite truck, which is only 2 miles away. If they can make it to the truck, the story can be inserted into the 5 p.m. broadcast. If not, the tape will have to be driven to the studio, meaning the reporter would record a voice-over for the 5 p.m. using his cellphone and drive aggressively to get back to the studio in time to get some video on the 5:30 p.m. and a package on the 6 p.m.

It's chaos, controlled chaos, in the newsroom. People are shouting, phones are ringing, and the monitors are turned up to see what the competition is doing. Despite the appearance of disorganization, everyone knows what to do, and they are focused on getting the programs on the air.

The studio director is in the newsroom, listening to what is going on because no matter how quickly Tamika revises the rundown, events are going to take place that won't be on the computer screen. She talks quietly with Pearl about graphics and calls the editing supervisor to check on progress on pieces for the 5 p.m. broadcast. Meanwhile, an operations assistant is making similar checks on the 5:30 p.m. rundown because the director, who is busy working on the 5 p.m. broadcast, handles both newscasts.

WHAT HAPPENS?

What happens? The news goes on. Even though the pros in the newsroom know there have been minor slip-ups and glitches, the viewers won't realize that stories are being finished at the last minute, changes are taking place literally minute-by-minute, and the "plan" for today's early block is no plan, it's flying by the seat of your pants.

The anchors sail through their broadcasts as if nothing untoward has occurred, even though the director and producer are talking into their earphones and the rundown is changing on their studio laptop screens. This is what anchorpeople do, they are rock steady in the midst of turmoil, informing the public while remaining calm.

To the viewer, it's a series of three stimulating, exciting, and informative news broadcasts, just like last evening and tomorrow evening. The viewers don't realize that large parts of the broadcast were unscripted, that the weather presenter had to condense her reports, and the sports anchor lost half of his allotted time. Everything goes off smoothly.

Behind the scenes, it's adrenalin, shouting, and even cheers when someone does the impossible. In the newsroom, everyone has one eye on the Channel 10 monitor

WHAT DOES A TV PRODUCER DO?

while noting what the competition is doing. Channel 10 wins hands down on the Interstate crash, with better video, better information, and clearer maps to show detours. The basketball practice dispute gets pushed down in the order, but it goes, and no one else has the story. Channel 7 whips the competition on the United Fund story by doing a really inciteful feature on how United Fund donations help a family in crisis. All the other channels covered the Fund luncheon remarks by the president of the First National Bank. Channel 26 went to the state capital for the conservation protest, but missed the Scargo trial verdict.

Does everyone in the newsroom sit there staring at the monitors? No. There's an 11 p.m. broadcast to produce, and the logistical moves necessary to making it an appealing broadcast must be made now. Assignments are made, editing instructions are issued for stories that will be reused from the early block, and an assistant producer is screening news feed material for the 11 p.m. Meanwhile, the producer is watching the raw video feed from the Interstate wreck, looking for excerpts that can be used on the 11 p.m. She must also decide whether or not to go with a live shot at the top of the 11 p.m. By then, much of the situation may be cleared up, and there may not be enough artificial lighting to make a live shot possible. This is a decision that can only be thought about at the moment, but soon she will have to make a "go or no go" decision, realizing the technical issues the crew faces, and knowing that almost all the on-scene crew is on overtime. To add to her concerns, she no longer has two night crews to assign to other stories.

This is what producing television news is about. Wouldn't you like to try it?

2

The Heart of the Newsroom: What People Use to Produce the News and How They Do It

Today's television news producer is the chief executive officer (CEO) of the newscast that succeeds or falters depending on how well the producer does her or his job. The producer works at a computer terminal, inputting plans and directions. These entries represent instructions the team will follow to produce the news program. Some of the instructions the producer enters will trigger automation programs that will carry out instructions without human intervention.

PRODUCERS, PLURAL

Before we move into a discussion of the computers systems used by producers, let's define some terms. There are several jobs that carry the title *producer,* and the titles describe different levels of responsibility. Typically the producer job titles are:

Executive Producer—The producer who is either in charge of all other producers, or in a very large organization, the lead producer on a major broadcast. The ABC program *Good Morning America* has an Executive Producer who is in overall charge of every aspect of the program.

Producer—The person in charge of a specific broadcast or several broadcasts. In the typical TV station, the producer of the 6 p.m. weekday local news would be the senior among equals in terms of experience and responsibility.

Field Producer—The person in charge of coverage on-scene of a news story. Field producers frequently do everything a reporter does, except appear on the air. They conduct interviews, do research, report, write scripts, coordinate with videographers, and supervise live transmissions. At the network level, a field producer may have several reporters, videographers, a dozen technicians and several remote trucks under their direction. At least one producer is assigned to each network bureau at The White House.

Associate Producer—Serves as either a backup to a producer, the producer of a major segment of a broadcast, or as producer of a fringe broadcast, such as the Sunday night 11 p.m. news. In a network or very large market operation, an associate producer might be responsible for a segment, specific stories within a news broadcast or might be assigned as a field producer. In the network environment, associate producers may be assigned to work with major anchorpersons or major correspondents.

Assistant Producer—This is usually the first step for someone striving to be a producer. Assistant producers help associate producers and producers by handling details including doing research, dealing with feeds, making telephone checks and doing telephone interviews. Talented assistant producers may substitute for broadcast producers when they are ill or on vacation.

Production Assistant—Entry level position for someone who aspires to be a producer, assignment editor, or writer. The basic "gofer" job in which you learn a lot and develop relationships that lead to promotion.

THE NEWSROOM AUTOMATION SYSTEM

The producer uses a computer-based newsroom automation system. There are fewer than a dozen brand-name systems commonly in use throughout the United States. The best known include Autocue from Autocue Holdings; Avid iNews from Avid Technology, Inc.; ENPS (Electronic News Production System) from The Associated Press; NewsKing from Comprompter; and "Open Media" from Dalet. Some newsrooms may have systems from AvStar, NewStar, NewsMaker, DCM (Data Center Management), BASYS or an earlier Associated Press system called NewsCenter.

Newsroom computer automation systems were developed to simplify the technical and operational parts of compiling a television news program, improve communication within the news operation, and replace human machine operators where possible. If you produce news for television, you will use a computer terminal linked to one of these newsroom automation systems.

THE HARDWARE

Most broadcast newsroom automation systems rely on personal computers (PCs) that are networked so that they can exchange information. Many systems interconnect their PCs by using Ethernet technology. Most software is based on operating and other systems from Microsoft Corporation.

Workstations are high-power desktop computers that offer extended capabilities to process and edit high quality audio and video. They also are used to create graphics, including virtual studios that appear real to viewers but are computer-created backdrops that are laid into the transmitted picture behind the anchors.

FIG. 2.1. An example of "virtual reality." The person in the picture appears to be reaching out of the frame to put a hat on a hat rack. The person is the only "real" object in the picture. Photo courtesy of RT-Set.

Laptops are heavily used by reporters and producers who do a great deal of traveling. They are especially handy for use in satellite newsgathering trucks and microwave units, where space is always tight. Some bureaus use laptops to save space or because they can be taken home. Some laptops can be used to edit video in the field.

Cellular telephone technology now makes it possible to connect laptops to the Internet and to the base computer. Experienced computer users who are frequent air travelers can be spotted in most airports because they carry an ordinary extension cord, which they plug into one of the airport's regular electrical outlets so that they can continue working after the battery has run down.

LINKED HARDWARE

A newsroom computer system is frequently linked to a number of production devices. The basic newsroom computer system is able to communicate with a wide spectrum of devices, including the:

Prompter—A name created by shortening the trademark name TelePrompTer. The prompter projects a large-type version of the script on a one-way mirror mounted in front of the camera(s) aimed at the anchorpersons. Air talent read off the mirror in order to maintain eye contact with viewers while the lens take their picture through the one-way mirror.

Character Generator [CG]—It electronically inserts text, such as the person's name and title, into the lower one third of the TV picture. The CG creates what are sometimes referred to as *supers* (from super-imposure), or subtitles. These are the ubiquitous names and titles that appear whenever a sound-on-tape (SOT) interview is run. The CG is sometimes referred to as the *Chyron* or *font* after leading manufacturers Chyron™ and Videfont™.

Still Store—An electronic file of "still" pictures. The still store electronically records images on tape or disk. Pictures of famous people, maps and certain titles are some of the images kept in the still store.

Chromakey™—An electronic device that makes the screen appear as if a still picture is located over the shoulder of the news anchor. Actually, there is nothing behind the anchor except a blue or other neutral color wall and the picture is inserted in the control room before the total image is sent to the transmitter. Typically these visuals contain a still picture (the governor), or a title (Governor Frank Reardon), or the first frame of a videotape, making it possible for the director to make a transition from the anchor shot to the next videotape story. Sometimes the "key" has two pictures, side by side. Producers call this a *double box*.

Closed Captioning—Computer software that translates the prompter output into a scrambled data transmission, which is unscrambled by a special black box receiver attached to the viewer's TV. The words being spoken appear in written form at the bottom of the TV screen. Closed-captioning was designed to benefit the hearing-impaired, but it is also used to promote learning English as a second language.

Camera Control—The unit that controls one or more automated robotic studio camera is linked to the newsroom computer system so that camera shots can be executed from cues, or switches, inserted in the script text.

Videotape or Disk Playback—The video and audio in most news broadcasts originates either from videotape that has been loaded into an automated videotape playback unit or from an optical or computer hard disk in a video server. The newsroom computer system can set up the order of events in a broadcast and have each element ready for the director to commit it to air.

Lights—It is possible to preset studio lighting clusters so that they can be turned on or off automatically by cues imbedded in the script.

"Virtual Reality"—A technology which makes it appear that the news anchors are located on a set, when they are really working in an empty studio. This technology may be linked to the newsroom computer system.

Feed Computer—The newsroom computer system is linked to devices that record incoming satellite and microwave feeds. The recording can be done either on videotape or digital disk. The feed computer makes certain the receiving antennas (dishes) are aimed at the right satellite at the right time, and then starts and stops the recording. Some feeds arrive on the Internet.

Production Control—The newsroom computer can control a news broadcast so that the director has all the elements ready, waiting for the command to execute. One of the devices involved is the routing switcher. Another is the main switching console where all the camera shots, device starts and stops, and visual effects are executed. Sometimes directors add digital video effects (DVEs) from the control room.

These are some of the hardware devices you will encounter as you learn about producing a news broadcast. Other devices which may not be linked to the newsroom computer system, but which you may encounter, included the Digital Video Effects (DVE) unit that creates special effects on the screen, and either linear (videotape) editing devices or digital (nonlinear) editing devices. These terms describe the technique used in editing news stories.

SOFTWARE

Software consists of a computer program that instructs the computer in accomplishing tasks, such as word-processing (typing) or creating a promotion visual, which is called a *graphic*. Computers can do a wide variety of jobs, depending on their configuration (the type of internal parts installed), the amount of memory installed, the running speed of the computer and the software installed.

Software is written in computer language, something learned in computer information systems classes. Writing software is a very specialized field, dominated by highly paid experts. Today's newsroom computer systems benefit from three decades of experience writing software to control the systems' hardware. Even with all the experience gained, some newsroom computer firms rely on packaged software they license from software companies to perform certain functions.

The complexity of software requires that some staff members have advanced knowledge of the inner workings of the newsroom computer system. When you get in trouble using the newsroom computer, you will call on the *system manager* or a *super-user* for help. These people have an aptitude for working with computers and usually receive special training from the system vendor.

Software is what you pay for when you purchase a newsroom computer system. Most vendors provide hardware recommendations because they know from experience that certain combinations of hardware (and some related software) work better. Vendors usually provide training when a new system is installed. Follow-up service, updates of the software and easy access to help technicians should be part of any newsroom computer system package.

THE COMPUTERIZED TV NEWSROOM

It's hard to picture a television newsroom without a computer system. A computer system promotes efficiency. Producers and editors can retrieve stories from writers and reporters and edit them without having to rely on messy pencil additions, or a confrontation with a writer who has been asked to rewrite a piece from scratch. If a rewrite is needed, the writer simply calls up the original copy from the computer's memory. Minor corrections can be made at the producer's desk.

Once the script is written, it is available to the video editors (working with videotape or digital video), the program producer and producers of other broadcasts, the assignment desk, the anchors, (who should preread), the director and the webmaster. Information contained in the script can be send to the prompter and closed-captioning devices, the printer (for hard copy), and the news library through the archives system. Hidden cues in the script can be sent to the automation system controller that actually runs production devices during a news broadcast.

Everyone who is authorized can access the item, while the producer uses a checks and balances system built into producer software to prevent unedited or unauthorized copy from getting on the air.

There's no need to carry hard copy across the room, or to send a fax to a bureau. Anyone connected to the system, who is authorized, may access the copy. This is a

FIG. 2.2. A newsroom computer system in a Washington, DC, news bureau. Courtesy AP ENPS.

necessity in today's newsroom, where several news broadcasts may be in production at the same time.

A computer system also saves steps and mounds of printer paper by taking in all the press agency feeds as data. Users view the lists of items received on their terminals, then they view or print out the stories they need. Some newer systems permit producers to view video on their terminals, which makes it much easier to select the video they want to use on a broadcast.

COMMUNICATION

A newsroom computer system simplifies and speeds up communication. Instead of having to type out notes or memos, newsroom staffers can write a note to one or more colleagues, and send the note on either the intranet or Internet.

The newsroom computer system has the ability to communicate with reporters in the field, or in bureaus. Staff members in a bureau are therefore privy to most of what is going on in the main newsroom. They know about policy statements and assignments. Reporters can keep producers and editors informed, and producers can coordinate events happening at remote locations. Editors, producers, and managers can tap into the system from home or a remote location and be updated. The most sophisticated systems permit crews to edit video in the field and send the stories, text and video, to the newsroom via the Internet.

The larger the organization, the more important communication becomes. The Cable News Network newsroom has a message line at the top of the terminal screen. It relays a steady stream of information, instructions and questions that may affect several hundred people at any one time. The message system saves a lot of phone calls and shouting across the newsroom. Major news organizations need to keep far-flung bureaus informed about current story emphases, and the bureaus need good communication systems in order to advise network headquarters about the stories they are covering. When the network goes on location for a major event, such as a visit by the president to Asian countries, the network can plug its traveling production units into the main computer system, which simplifies logistical communication and keeps everyone updated on breaking news stories that may impact the remote coverage.

ORGANIZING

A computer system lends itself to organizing important data. A news department can keep track of future assignments as well as check on who is where at the moment. Old scripts which are archived in the system become sources because they can be easily retrieved. Everyone involved with a particular news program can take a look at the producer's rundown and get an idea what needs to be done for the broadcast. Shared information helps to avoid duplications in other news broadcasts.

Routine business functions, such as personnel schedules, lend themselves to computerization. Computers are wonderful for handling telephone calls. The person receiving the call can switch to the message screen and type out the caller's message if the recipient isn't in the newsroom. Viewer inquiries or legal questions can be answered quickly when scripts, rundowns, and video can be accessed from the files.

Most newsroom systems are set up so that staff members are able to access parts of the system from home. This means staff members can read in on what is going on from home, which makes the transition into the ongoing work flow smoother. Managers can monitor what is going on, and send notes or comments when needed.

Another element to organization is keeping track of vital information. This can include a telephone directory of frequently called numbers, maps of the coverage area, emergency plans, serial numbers of equipment (for insurance and customs), and mileage elapsed on mobile unit tires.

AUTOMATION

The newsroom computer system's greatest utility is its automation function. Imagine you are writing a TV news script. Traditionally TV news scripts have two columns. Audio and video instructions, subtitles, camera switches, and other production notes are typed in the left column. The right column contains the text.

Prior to the development of automation if you typed: *SUPER Mayor James Baldwin* on the left side of a script, the following actions had to take place:

1. Someone had to look in a slide file and see it contained a super slide that said *Mayor James Baldwin* was in the file. If it was, the slide was taken out, and put in a slide holder with other super slides. Before the broadcast, the slide holder and a list of the slides to be used had to be delivered to the projectionist, who inserted the slides in a special slide projector. Just before the slide was due to be shown on the air, the director would glance up at the monitor that showed previews of slides, and then give the instruction to *take super*. The super would be manually inserted into the picture by punching a button on the console, and a few seconds later, it would be deleted by punching a second button.
2. If no slide existed, an artist had to create the artwork and shoot a slide before the process could move forward.

Today, here's what happens:

When you type in the super, you insert a number, for the visual if it is in a computer file, along with a cue to tell the character generator (CG) to find and load the super. The super comes up on the preview monitor automatically, awaiting only a push of a button to insert it into the on-air picture. Alternatively, the super can be edited into a story package prior to the broadcast, so all the director has to do is "commit" the story to air by pushing a start button.

If the super isn't already stored in the CG, you can call up a template on your computer screen. All you do is fill in the title and name, and the software creates a super and sends it to CG.

This is one small example of what automation can do. Information can be inserted in scripts and in the producer's computer rundown that triggers all of the devices used in producing a news broadcast. These include cameras, the Chromakey, the character generator, the still-store, the digital video effects device, audio, remote cameras, and lights. Each device is ready to execute its next job and awaits the director's manual instruction to commit it to air.

In the most sophisticated applications, automation technology can run a whole broadcast without intervention by a director. One way to do this is to prerecord each element of the broadcast, and then give the automation system a set of instructions (rundown) describing every function that has to take place. The automation system then withdraws each completed element from a computer server (large hard-disk computer) and plays the element on-cue, on time. Technology similar to this is used at several Time-Warner Cable all-news channels.

THE SKILLS YOU NEED

Most journalism students have listened to "war stories" told by faculty, grads back for homecoming, and visiting professionals. Yes, things were tough when they got started, but the technology demands were different, and possibly less daunting.

The wide availability of technology and the broad range of costs for acquiring technology are impacting students. Let's do a comparison. The journalism student entering television journalism in the late 1960s typically had to know how to do the following in a small market (100 plus, and many even larger).

Then

- Type on a manual typewriter. Learn to insert carbon paper between two pieces of typing paper.
- Write a television news story. (Many beginners in television had already acquired commercial radio news experience).
- Report from the field. This consisted of recording a voice over, either from the field, or in the studio.
- Report on camera in the field. If you made a mistake, you did a retake on film. Even long on-camera pieces were memorized, paragraph by paragraph, and then shot in several takes.
- Shoot silent film, mainly in daylight, using a spring-wound camera, and if one were lucky, a light meter to adjust lens settings.
- Shoot sound film. A maybe, depending on station policy, and whether or not the station used one-person bands (reporters who shot film and re-

ported by doing sound interviews from behind the camera and then filming themselves doing short on-camera introductions).
- Live on-camera—mainly weekend anchoring, for reporters who showed talent or had more experience than their colleagues.

Now

- Type on a computer terminal, know basic PC functions and how to use a Windows program. Be able to save copy and send it to a printer. Be able to perform computer functions such as searching the archives, sending e-mail, doing an Internet search, fill out an assignment form, or transfer data to the producer's desk.
- Write a television story with imbedded cues for automation. Send the story to the producer for review. Stories are more complex because the graphic devices are more sophisticated.
- Prepare character generator titles. Run the CG during a broadcast.
- Search the still store file.

FIG. 2.3. A videographer shooting action during the Second Gulf War (2003) in Iraq. Several news agencies used highly compact, laptop-computer based video editing and satellite transmission units to send coverage of the war from the front lines. Photo courtesy of Livewire, Switzerland.

- Report from the field using a two-way radio or a cellphone. Record voice-overs in the studio.
- Report on camera in the field. The recording medium is videotape or a digital medium, which is about as complicated as working with film, but it is possible to review your standups and interviews.
- Report LIVE on-camera in the field. This is daunting, especially for a beginner just out of school, with no commercial experience. Even stations in very, very small markets can afford microwave technology to do live coverage. Sometimes your work is fed to the network news cooperative, so all your novice mistakes are available throughout the region.
- Report live and chat intelligently with the anchors.
- Shoot video and edit video.
- Edit video from your terminal, and prepare a shot list.

The point is this: A trainee journalist in the 21st century is going to have to be able to do more, do it faster, do it more professionally than those entering the field two generations ago.

CONCLUSION

Every new broadcast journalist needs to be familiar with personal computers, not only to carry out internships and to enter the world of work, but as a way to position themselves for advancement as they acquire experience. The greater your knowledge of computers, computer hardware, software and programming, the better the opportunities that will be available to you in the broadcast news business.

3

The Producer's Desk: Where it All Comes Together

The producer's desk is one of two "hubs" in a television newsroom. The other hub is the control room where the news program is assembled and transmitted.

A popular term used to describe the producer's working area is *pod*. Many broadcast newsrooms put the producer's desk, with its computer terminal, multiline telephone, and other communication devices at the focus of a cluster of desks and workstations, so that there can be both spoken and visual contact among members of the team. A producer generally has a high degree of contact with the assignment desk, which sends out reporter–videographer crews and keeps track of breaking stories. Other people who communicate frequently with the producer include, associate or assistant producers, writers, researchers, production assistants, video editors, the satellite feed coordinator, the operations supervisor, graphics personnel, the promotion staff, and as the newscast time approaches, reporters, field producers, anchors, and directors.

The producer has a very high level of access to the newsroom computer system, and usually can see any information that relates to putting together the broadcast. The producer gathers a great deal of information and develops the *rundown* or *running-order*, a very structured document that is a production road-map describing exactly what is needed, and when it is needed in the news broadcast. However, the rundown is simply the scheduled plan of the newscast. If something important happens suddenly, the producer can and will rearrange the rundown. The program's director uses the rundown to call for camera shots and order devices operated while the program is going out over the air.

ASSEMBLING THE RUNDOWN

Any broadcast program can be described to a professional in terms of two elements: the **format** and the **rundown**. The format comes up as a template or preprinted information every time you open a new rundown.

FIG. 3.1. A producer and his team are clustered in a "pod" at WTVT-TV in Tampa. Photo by P. Keirstead, courtesy of WTVT-TV, Tampa, Florida.

The format is a document that lists the constants about a program. By *constants,* I mean the elements that do not change for a specific program, such as the Monday through Friday 6 p.m. news. They include:

1. The **teaser**—this is the live and/or taped insert that is usually shown during the 2 minutes leading up to a news broadcast's starting time. Typically each anchor will read one headline, the weather forecaster will summarize the weather highlights in a phrase, and the sports anchor will read a sports headline.
2. The **opening**—this is a preproduced videotape or disk file that usually includes dynamic video and video graphics and mentions the station's channel number, news slogan, or both. These openings are frequently produced by companies that specialize in creating promotional opens and closes. Copies of the open and close are stored in the automated tape playback unit or the video server, whichever is used to send video to air.
3. **Live open**—some stations follow with another round-robin introducing the anchors, weathercaster and sports personality. The copy reads slightly differently, but this resembles the teaser. Some stations go right into the news, usually with both anchors reading the beginning paragraphs of the first story. A more dramatic approach is to start with news video.

First News at Five   Producer Rundown

Date: Friday, April 17, 1998   Time: 5:00:00 PM   Out Time: 5:30:00 PM

Page	Story/Slug	OnCam	Tape#	Type	Length	Front	Back	Live
A01	5p Short Open	--	Open ID	SOT	00:10	5:00:00 P	5:00:10 P	
A02	5p Video Tease	Steve; Myra	021	VO	00:10	5:00:10 P	5:00:20 P	
A03	5P blimp crash folo	Myra	009,010	VO/SOT	00:40	5:00:20 P	5:00:30 P	
A04	5p air show preps intro	Steve		RDR	00:15	5:01:00 P	5:01:10 P	
A05	5p air show live	Ethan	TAPE 009	live/pkg	02:00	5:01:15 P	5:01:25 P	
A06	5p air show schedule	Steve		MATTE	00:25	5:03:15 P	5:03:25 P	
A07	5p harambee festival	Myra	013,017	VO/SOT	00:40	5:03:40 P	5:03:50 P	
A08	5p harambee schedule	Myra		MATTE	00:20	5:04:20 P	5:04:30 P	
A09	5p turkey bills	Steve	022	VO	00:25	5:04:40 P	5:04:50 P	
A11	5p boot camps	Steve	004	VO	00:25	5:05:05 P	5:05:15 P	
A13	5p disability fraud folo	Myra	023,026	VO/SOT	00:40	5:05:30 P	5:05:40 P	
A14	5p elderly drivers	Myra	014	PKG	00:40	5:06:10 P	5:06:20 P	
A15	5p racy shirt	Steve	027	VO	00:20	5:06:50 P	5:07:00 P	
A16	5p Intro First Wx	Myra; Steve	--		00:10	5:07:10 P	5:07:20 P	
A17	5p First Weather	Siler	--		00:45	5:07:20 P	5:07:30 P	
A18	5p Bump One	Steve; Myra	Bump 1	VO	00:20	5:08:05 P	5:08:15 P	
A19	5p Re-Open	--	Re-Open		00:20	5:08:25 P	5:08:35 P	
B00	--- B R E A K ---				02:00	5:08:45 P	5:08:55 P	
B01	5p America Tonight	myra	--		00:01	5:10:45 P	5:10:55 P	
B01.5	5p postal shooting	Myra	029	VO	00:20	5:10:46 P	5:10:56 P	
B02	5p nashville tornado	Myra	030	VO	00:20	5:11:06 P	5:11:16 P	
B03	5p shuttle crew	Steve	031	VO	00:20	5:11:26 P	5:11:36 P	
B04	5p lewinsky	Steve	032	VO	00:20	5:11:46 P	5:11:56 P	
B05	5p Bump Two	Myra; Steve	Bump 2	VO	00:20	5:12:06 P	5:12:16 P	
C00	--- B R E A K ---				02:10	5:12:26 P	5:12:36 P	
C01	5p Weather	Wx		Chroma	03:30	5:14:36 P	5:14:46 P	
C02	5p Six Oclock Tease	Myra; Kelly	006 HB-98-01 020	MATTE	00:37	5:18:06 P	5:18:16 P	
C03	5p Bump Three	Steve, Myra	Bump 3	VO	00:20	5:18:43 P	5:18:53 P	
D00	--- B R E A K ---				02:00	5:19:03 P	5:19:13 P	
D01	5p Stocks	Matte			00:10	5:21:03 P	5:21:13 P	
D02	5p Sports live intro	St/Myra/Block	--		03:00	5:21:13 P	5:21:23 P	
D03	5p					5:24:13 P	5:24:23 P	
D04	5p					5:24:13 P	5:24:23 P	
D05	5p					5:24:13 P	5:24:23 P	
D06	5p					5:24:13 P	5:24:23 P	
D07	5p					5:24:13 P	5:24:23 P	
D08	5p Sports Tag	St/Myra/Block	--		00:15	5:24:13 P	5:24:23 P	
D10	5p smart woman	Myra	25	PKG	01:47	5:24:28 P	5:24:38 P	
D11	5p Bump Four	Steve; Myra	Bump 4	VO	00:20	5:26:15 P	5:26:25 P	
E00	--- B R E A K ---				02:10	5:26:35 P	5:26:45 P	
E01	5p Final Weather	Myra; Steve; SILER	--		00:20	5:28:45 P	5:28:55 P	
E02	5p red kangaroos	Myra	002	VO	00:25	5:29:05 P	5:29:15 P	
E03	5p Goodbye	Steve; Myra; Block; Siler			00:20	5:29:30 P	5:29:40 P	

FIG. 3.2.   Producer rundown.

4. **Outline**—the format is also a structural outline of the program. It includes such critical information as the total running time, the elements or sections, the number of commercial breaks and the length of each, how each section or *block* of the program is designated. One format might call for all local stories in the first section, a switch to world and national news in the second, longer form features including business news in the third, weather in the fourth, sports in the fifth, and a feature and a lighter story in the final section. The content and the exact time of each section would change practically every night, but the type of information contained in the block would not change.

5. **Bumpers**—these are the "stay-tuned" reminders that promote upcoming stories just before commercial breaks.

6. **Blocks**—the placement of the blocks within a format is a critical decision that is usually made at the executive level on advice from the news director because the choice of content of these blocks equates to the ratings. In general, ratings for television programs are gathered for 15-minute segments. So, if you are producing a 30-minute news program, the critical times for you are the open, the midpoint, and the close. The open, you hope, will keep the attention of people who were watching the preceding program and convince others to click over to your news. If there is a radical change in audience during the program it would likely be recorded during the midpoint of the program. Because news audience ratings analyze total people watching, men watching, women watching, different age groups watching (and sometimes other demographics), advertisers want to be certain that they are not only getting the raw numbers they desire, but the right *demographics,* which is the right mix of gender, age and spending ability.

You may have wondered why the weather forecast frequently hits air at 13 minutes after the hour. Weather usually tests stronger on female demographics than sports. Because ratings are cumulative, television executives want to be certain the larger audience, a mixture of women and men, is recorded in the second quarter hour before some women drop out because they may not be interested in sports. You might want to time a few local news broadcasts, and see how the programs are formatted.

7. **Closing**—some stations purchase highly produced closings, others close on a locally produced sequence. Most closing promote the next program or the next news broadcast.

BLOCKS

The typical news program is divided in sections, called *blocks*. The first block of a half hour is critical because it sets the tone for the rest of the broadcast. A station with news programs at 5 p.m., 5:30 p.m., and 6 p.m. is going to design the blocks in each half hour differently, based on the audience at the time.

> 5:00 p.m.—Many stations will lead with a national or international story in the first block at 5 p.m., unless there is a local story of overwhelming importance.

THE PRODUCERS DESK   33

The argument for this approach is that the viewer needs a quick summary of all the major news, and the network broadcast of national and international news won't be on for 90 minutes.

5:30 p.m.—A local lead may be favored at 5:30 p.m. It will probably be different from the 6 p.m. lead because the 6 p.m. program is likely to be higher rated and is adjacent to the 6:30 p.m. network news. The 5:30 p.m. lead can be a different story, or a different version of a very important local story. If the local story broke late in the afternoon, the producer may choose to do a long, detailed version, leaving a tighter but highly produced "package" for the 6 p.m. broadcast.

6:00 p.m.—Many stations favor a local lead, usually the top local story, or a late-breaking story. National and international coverage, which is usually brief, will be relegated to the second block, if there is any national/international news in the broadcast.

Selecting a lead story requires thought and analysis. In some cases, a breaking story would lead. A local bank was held up at 4 p.m. If police intervened and captured the robber, it may be worthy of a lead. But what if the robber did not show a weapon and walked out with what appears to be a small sum of money? So recent occurrence alone does not make a lead, unless station policy calls for a late-breaking crime, accident, or fire story when available. A major national story, such as a breakthrough in medical research, especially if it has a local tie-in, might make a good lead for some broadcasts. In the morning, a traffic tie-up might lead a half hour of the morning show.

THE RUNDOWN

The **Rundown** is the list of events and sources for a specific broadcast, such as Thursday, June 7th from 6 p.m. to 7 p.m. The format is incorporated into the computer program used by the producer, so it doesn't have to be typed into the computer each time a producer starts working on a specific broadcast.

The rundown is laid out when the system is installed, but can be modified by a qualified "super-user." The producer keyboards in each story or event that is scheduled, along with relevant information about sources and production devices needed. Anytime a change is made to rundowns, the computer recalculates the time accumulated, and compares the total time available to the time allocated for stories.

At Fox-affiliate WTVT-TV in Tampa, Florida, the top row of the computer screen had the following entries:

PAGE   ANCHOR   FRAME   SLUG   VIDEO   TIME   BKT

PAGE—Done consecutively, but each section gets its own set of numbers: Section One is 1-19, Section 2 is 20-29, etc. If a section runs out of numbers, an A can be added after the number, as in 7A. Therefore, item 33 is the third item in Section Three.

News 8 WMTW at 6   Producer Rundown

Date: Thursday, June 28, 2001   Time: 05:59:00 PM   Out Time: 06:27:50 PM

Page	Story/Slug	Type	Writer	Editor	OnCam	Length	Back
A01	NEWS 8 OPEN	SOT				00:10	5:58:43 PM
A02	COMMTEL	2-SHOT	DykB		DoughertyJ; LauberJ; DoughertyJ	00:23	5:58:53 PM
A03	TOSS TO BOB	NITELINE	DykB		DoughertyJ	00:05	5:59:16 PM
A04	V-COMMTEL	CONGRE	DykB		DykB	00:44	5:59:21 PM
A05	S-COMMTEL	DIS/SOT/	DykB		DykB	00:35	6:00:05 PM
A06	TOSS BACK	NITELINE	DykB		DoughertyJ; DoughertyJ	00:05	6:00:40 PM
A07	GO FISH	SOT/TAG	Wetherbeel		DoughertyJ	00:34	6:00:45 PM
A08	VISHAY SPRAGUE	VO/TOP	Wetherbeel		DoughertyJ	00:20	6:01:19 PM
A09	MAINE.POLY	WIPE/VO	Wetherbeel		DoughertyJ	00:20	6:01:39 PM
A10	BASE.CLOSURES	VO	Wetherbeel		LauberJ	00:20	6:01:59 PM
A11	FIRST LOOK WEATHER	2-SHOT	Wetherbeel		LauberJ; DoughertyJ	00:10	6:02:19 PM
A12	WX: first look	WX/MONI			McNallyL	00:30	6:02:29 PM
A13	PAMELA WEBB	2-SHOT	YoungC		DoughertyJ; LauberJ	00:14	6:02:59 PM
A14	P-PAMELA WEBB	PKG	YoungC			02:22	6:03:13 PM
A15	JALBERT/SEX.OF	VO	Wetherbeel		LauberJ	00:27	6:05:35 PM
A16	PRE-RELEASE.CI	RDR	McClellandl		DoughertyJ	00:15	6:06:02 PM
A17	TOSS TO KATIE	NITELINE	McClellandl		DoughertyJ	00:05	6:06:17 PM
A18	V-PRE-RELEASE.	CONGRE	McClellandl		McClellandK	00:30	6:06:22 PM
A19	S-PRE-RELEASE.	DIS/SOT/	McClellandl		McClellandK	00:30	6:06:52 PM
A20	TOSS BACK	NITELINE	McClellandl		DoughertyJ	00:05	6:07:22 PM
A21	TRESCOTT FIRE	MAP/TAG	Wetherbeel		DoughertyJ	00:25	6:07:27 PM
A22	S.PORTLAND.RO.	VO/DIS	CanlasE		DoughertyJ	00:20	6:07:52 PM
A23	S-S.PORTLAND.R	DIS/SOT/	CanlasE		DoughertyJ	00:20	6:08:12 PM
A24	LEWISTON.WATE	VO	Wetherbeel		LauberJ	00:20	6:08:32 PM
A25	TSE 1	VO/VO	Wetherbeel		LauberJ; DoughertyJ	00:15	6:08:52 PM

FIG. 3.3. Producer rundown.

News 8 WMTW at 6 — Producer Rundown

Date: Thursday, June 28, 2001   Time: 05:59:00 PM   Out Time: 06:27:50 PM

Page	Story/Slug	Type	Writer	Editor	OnCam	Length	Back
B00	--- B R E A K ---	************				01:55	6:09:07 PM
B01	AMERICAN.EAGL	VO/DIS	Wetherbeel		DoughertyJ	00:12	6:11:02 PM
B02	S-AMERICAN.EA(	DIS/SOT	Wetherbeel		DoughertyJ	00:20	6:11:14 PM
B03	JETPORT.WEBSI'	SOT/TAG	Wetherbeel		DoughertyJ; ------------	00:30	6:11:34 PM
B04	S.PORTLAND.CO!	VO/TOP	Wetherbeel		LauberJ	00:20	6:12:04 PM
B05	WEDDING.REGIS	VO/DIS	BoxerE		LauberJ	00:20	6:12:24 PM
B06	S-WEDDING.REG	DIS/SOT/\	BoxerE		LauberJ	00:20	6:12:44 PM
B07	TSE 2: wx bump	WX BUMP	Wetherbeel		LauberJ; DoughertyJ	00:20	6:13:04 PM
C00	--- B R E A K ---	************				01:40	6:13:24 PM
C02	WEATHER INTRO	3-SHOT			LauberJ; DoughertyJ	00:15	6:15:04 PM
C03	WEATHERCAST	WX WALL			McNallyL	03:00	6:15:19 PM
C04	TOSS BACK	3-SHOT			LauberJ; DoughertyJ	00:15	6:18:19 PM
C05	TSE 3:sports	VO/VO			DoughertyJ; LauberJ	00:15	6:18:34 PM
D00	--- B R E A K ---	************				01:40	6:18:49 PM
D02	SPORTS INTRO	3-SHOT			DoughertyJ; LauberJ	00:15	6:20:29 PM
D03	SPORTSCAST	RDR			KarkosN	03:30	6:20:44 PM
D04	GPO RDR	RDR			PearchM		6:24:14 PM
D05	TOSS TO TRAVIS	NITELINE					6:24:14 PM
D06	golf vo	STOOL/V(			LeeT		6:24:14 PM
D07	golf cg	WIPE/CG					6:24:14 PM
D08	SEA DOGS RDR	RDR			PearchM		6:24:14 PM
D09	RED SOX	VO			PearchM		6:24:14 PM
D10	FLORIE SOT	SOT			PearchM		6:24:14 PM
D11	GWYNN VO	VO/DIS			PearchM		6:24:14 PM
D12	GWYNN SOT	DIS/SOT					6:24:14 PM

FIG. 3.3. (continued)   (continued on next page)

News 8 WMTW at 6 — Producer Rundown

Date: Thursday, June 28, 2001 Time: 05:59:00 PM Out Time: 06:27:50 PM

Page	Story/Slug	Type	Writer	Editor	OnCam	Length	Back
D13	WIMBLEDON	RDR			PearchM		6:24:14 PM
D14	NBA DRAFT	VO/TOP					6:24:14 PM
D15	TAG SPORTS	3-SHOT				00:15	6:24:14 PM
D16	TSE 4	VO/TOP	Wetherbeel		LauberJ	00:10	6:24:29 PM
E00	---BREAK---	************				01:40	6:24:39 PM
E01	COMING UP @ 11	VO/VO/VO	McCauslan(		DoughertyJ	00:25	6:26:19 PM
E02	FINAL WEATHER	WX MAP/4-DA			LauberJ	00:25	6:26:44 PM
E03	SEEDS OF PEACE	NAT/VO	Wetherbeel		LauberJ	00:25	6:27:09 PM
E04	GOODBYES	4-SHOT			LauberJ; DoughertyJ	00:06	6:27:34 PM
E05	** DROP LIGHTS **	BUMP				00:05	6:27:40 PM
E06	COPYRIGHT	GRAPHIC				00:05	6:27:45 PM
E07	**********************	************			******************		6:27:50 PM
E08	TOPICAL A :15	RDR	HammondE		LauberJ		6:27:50 PM
E09	TOPICAL B :15	RDR	HammondE		LauberJ		6:27:50 PM
E10	TOPICAL C :15	RDR	Wetherbeel		DoughertyJ		6:27:50 PM
E11	11 PM :15 TEASE	RDR	McCauslan(		DoughertyJ		6:27:50 PM
E12	11 PM :15 TEASE	RDR	McCauslan(		DoughertyJ		6:27:50 PM
E13	11 PM :04 ID	RDR	McCauslan(		DoughertyJ		6:27:50 PM
E14	11 PM :04 ID	RDR	McCauslan(		DoughertyJ		6:27:50 PM
E15							6:27:50 PM
E16							6:27:50 PM

FIG. 3.3. (continued)

ANCHOR—Initials. The entry KD/2 means an opening shot with both anchors, K and D on camera. The anchors have to know when they are on camera and the director needs to know what shot to set up.

FRAME—Live = live, DB = double box (each anchor appears to be in a separate screen within a screen, 2-shot (two anchors in same shot)

SLUG—Story name such as ISRAEL CRISIS, referring to a story about the on-going conflict between Israel and its Palestinian neighbors.

VIDEO—Source of the picture. SOT = sound-on-tape SOT-KEY = sound on tape begins as a Chromakey [picture behind or over the shoulder of the anchor] and then crossfades into actual tape [full screen]. VO = voice over, the anchor reads over the video (which may have background sound) PKG-CG-BAN 8060 = A fully produced "package" story which needs a Character Generator title "Ban 8060."

TIME—The first entry is how long the items runs, the BKT entry is "back-time," or how much time remains, which is a way of making sure a program ends on time.

Most rundown programs provide front and back timing. Front timing would show how long each item is and list its desired start or "hit" time. Backtiming calculates how much time should remain in the program at the conclusion of any one story. Backtiming is important in order to get the program off the air on

Rundown for Midday - Apella (2004-01-05) Printed at 10:24 AM on 1/05/2004 Job Page: 1 of 1
Print Format: Producer Rundown by connie

ITEM	SLUG	TALENT	FORMAT	TAPE	ERT	SOT	TOTAL	HIT TIME
					00:00		16:27	12:43:39 am
	Segment 1				00:00		04:35	12:43:39 am
1	IRAQ	CANDICE	VO-|PKG-	INTRO||RA	00:18	01:45	02:03	12:43:39 am
2	VOTE	Bill	VO-	VOTE	00:22		00:22	12:45:42 am
3	PEACE	CANDICE	VO-	Peace	00:20		00:20	12:46:04 am
4	TRACTOR	CANDICE	VO-	Tractor	00:34		00:34	12:46:24 am
5	JONES	CANDICE	VO-	Jones	00:45		00:45	12:46:58 am
6	BUMP 1	CANDICE	RDR		00:11		00:11	12:47:43 am
	BREAK 1				00:00	00:20	00:20	12:47:54 am
	Segment 2				00:00		03:40	12:48:14 am
7	PAWS	CANDY	INTERV		00:03	03:00	03:03	12:48:14 am
8	BUMP 2	CANDY|TED			00:07	00:10	00:17	12:51:17 am
	BREAK 2				00:00	00:20	00:20	12:51:34 am
	Segment 3				00:00		05:03	12:51:54 am
9	WEATHER	TED	GFX		00:00	03:00	03:00	12:51:54 am
10	MR. FOOD	TED/CANDY	PKG-	MrFood	00:06	01:38	01:44	12:54:54 am
11	BUMP 3	CANDICE	RDR		00:09		00:09	12:56:38 am
	BREAK 3				00:00	00:10	00:10	12:56:47 am
	Segment 4				00:00		02:15	12:56:57 am
12	ILLNESS	CANDICE	VO-	illness	00:19		00:19	12:56:57 am
13	HORMONE	CANDICE	VO-	8026	00:27		00:27	12:57:16 am
14	BUMP 4				00:05	00:04	00:09	12:57:43 am
	BREAK 4				00:00	01:20	01:20	12:57:52 am
	Segment 5				00:00		00:54	12:59:12 am
15	WX CHECK2	CANDICE|TED	GFX		00:04	00:30	00:34	12:59:12 am
16	GOODBYE				00:05		00:05	12:59:46 am
17	CREDITS		SOT-		00:00	00:15	00:15	12:59:51 am
					00:00		00:00	1:00:06 pm

FIG. 3.4. NewsKing producer rundown. Courtesy of Comprompter Newsroom & Automation Systems.

time. Producers need both sets of numbers, which they compare with real time as the program is being broadcast. The producer can eliminate items, or stretch the weather forecaster's section (which is done extemporaneously or ad lib) in order to come out on time.

There can be problems with backtiming programs for computers, as some software does not cope well with live shots and ad lib segments. Producers rely on many stratagems to time to the end of programs. Some trust stopwatches and digital timers, others do math on paper, a few use special computer programs.

One mental hurdle inexperienced producers run into is remembering that time is based on 6 not 10. Therefore 60 seconds plus 60 seconds is 120 seconds but it is not one minute plus 20 seconds, it is 2 minutes. Producers in training should discuss backtiming methods with experienced pros and develop a system that works. Most experienced producers give one warning: Do not rely totally on the computer!

Some hints about backtiming:

- Time is based on 60, not 100, 60 seconds equals 1 minute, two units of 60 seconds (120 seconds) are 2 minutes.
- Do the math ahead of time, know when you're targeted to hit a break.
- Do backtiming calculations on paper.
- Anticipate hit times for commercial breaks or other key elements in a program. If you arrive at the hit time, you're OK. If you're early, something has to stretch in the next segment. If you're late, something has to be cut or eliminated.
- Experienced producers plan to have two or three short items and some ad lib time for the anchors inserted in the next-to-last and last segments so that 15, 20, or 30 second overruns can be overcome by dropping a short item. One ad lib possibility for the anchors is to promote the upcoming broadcast or an upcoming newscast.
- For a news broadcast, figure the latest time possible time to start the final sequence to get to a break or the end of the program. For example:
    Off time: 5:28:50
    Closing Audio/video—:30—start at 5:28:20
    Anchor "Goodbyes"—:20—start at 5:28:00
    Final Weather Wrap—:20—start at 5:27:40.
So no matter what, you have to begin the process of getting out of the broadcast no later than 5:27:50.
- If you are familiar with computer spreadsheet programs such as Microsoft Excel, an experienced, computer-savvy producer can show you how to create your own backtiming program.

Many rundown programs include a status column that tells the producer which stories have not come in, which have been written and edited (video), which have been approved by the editor or producer, and flash warnings if copy is withdrawn for rewriting or correction.

The number of devices listed, such as character generators, still stores, and so forth, is dependent on whether the station has facilities to preproduce a story with all the elements included, or whether the system, or a person, has to add character generator or still store images as the piece is being played out to air.

The rundown undergoes constant revision. In the hour before the broadcast it is printed and sent to the places and people where it is used in paper form: the control room, the director, the anchors, technical departments. However, nothing says the rundown can't be changed and it is not unusual for programs and rundowns to be changed during a broadcast, especially at stations with the live capabilities. The rundown can be called up on several terminals, so that key positions can see the changes.

There are differences in how programs are produced, according to market size, staff size, time of day, day of the week, and whether the production is for a local station or a network. Some stations have an executive producer who is responsible for overseeing all news programs, in others, the news director does this. At the networks, there are producers assigned to individual stories and segments and a producer and an executive producer for each major news program.

A MORNING PRODUCER AT WORK

WTXL-TV: An Example

A morning producer for WTXL-TV, an ABC affiliate in Tallahassee, Florida, a 100-plus market (the number 1 market has the greatest number of potential viewers, market rankings are assigned higher numbers as the potential audience decreases) faces many challenges. At the time of our interview, the morning producer was responsible for the 5:30 to 7 a.m. news broadcasts, and the 12 p.m. 30-minute broadcast. The producer was working in her first job and had been with the station 2 months, following graduation from the journalism program at Northwestern University.

She arrived at work at 2 a.m. and spent the early morning hours rewriting and recutting stories from the night before for use on the morning news, which was staffed by a news anchor and a weather/features anchor, who was a meteorologist.

She started working on the noon program during the 7 a.m. to 9 a.m. hours, while the anchors did network cut-ins in ABC's *Good Morning America*. Much of the noon content was rewritten and recut stories, with the option of picking up items from the ABC NewsOne feed to affiliates.

The news hole or time to be filled averaged 13 to 14 minutes, over-all, but the actual fresh news portion averaged 6½ minutes. There were commitments to use a weather segment, taped entertainment and medical packages, and a syndicated "Smart Woman" feature, which was voiced by one of the station's anchors.

On this day the producer had the possibility of getting a live feed from ABC News via satellite from Nashville, Tennessee, which had experienced extensive damage from a tornado the evening before. Although Tennessee was two states

News at Noon

Producer Rundown

Date: Friday, April 17, 1998   Time: 12:00:00 PM   Out Time: 12:30:00 PM

Page	Story/Slug	OnCam	Tape#	Type	Length	Front	Back	Live
A01	12n Short Open				00:10	12:00:00 P	12:00:48 P	
A02	12n Video Tease	Tammy	bb1		00:12	12:00:10 P	12:00:58 P	
A03	12n Tornadoes	Tammy	????	live/pkg	02:20	12:00:22 P	12:01:10 P	
A04	12n Toxic Spill CT	Tammy	010	VO	00:25	12:03:02 P	12:03:30 P	
A05	12n Robbery	Tammy	120	VO/MAT	00:32	12:03:28 P	12:03:55 P	
A06	12n Urban Growth	Tammy	002 003	VO/SOT	00:44	12:04:02 P	12:04:27 P	
A07	12n Tally Homeless	Tammy	004	VO	00:20	12:04:48 P	12:05:11 P	
A08	12n FL Budget	Tammy	021	VO	00:16	12:05:06 P	12:05:31 P	
A09	12n Wine By Mail	Tammy	009	VO	00:26	12:05:22 P	12:05:47 P	
A10	12n Paula Jones	Tammy	012	VO	00:15	12:05:41 P	12:06:13 P	
A11	12n Ireland Talks	Tammy	008	VO	00:23	12:05:56 P	12:06:28 P	
A12	12nOldestPerson	Tammy	020	VO	00:14	12:06:18 P	12:06:51 P	
A13	12n Intro First Wx	Tammy; Glenn			00:10	12:06:44 P	12:07:05 P	
A14	12Traffic/Wx Tease	Glenn			00:30	12:06:54 P	12:07:15 P	
A15	12n Bump One	Glenn	bump 1		00:19	12:07:24 P	12:07:45 P	
A16	Re-Open				00:20	12:07:43 P	12:08:04 P	
B00	--- B R E A K ---				02:05	12:07:59 P	12:08:24 P	
B01	One Year ago		005		00:10	12:10:04 P	12:10:29 P	
B02	12n Shuttle	Tammy	017	VO	00:28	12:10:19 P	12:10:39 P	
B03	12n Weather	Glenn		Chroma	03:30	12:10:53 P	12:11:07 P	
B04	12n 5/6 Tease	Tammy		MATTE	00:27	12:14:49 P	12:14:37 P	
B05	12n smart woman	Tammy	25	PKG	01:48	12:15:14 P	12:15:04 P	
B07	12n Bump Two	Tammy; Glenn	BUMP 2		00:22	12:17:02 P	12:16:52 P	
C00	--- B R E A K ---				02:35	12:17:16 P	12:17:14 P	
C01	12 Bump In				00:10	12:19:51 P	12:19:49 P	
C02	12n Poison Caution	Tammy	018	PKG	01:27	12:19:52 P	12:19:59 P	
C04	12n Bump Three	Tammy	Bump 3		00:25	12:21:19 P	12:21:26 P	
D00	--- B R E A K ---				02:05	12:21:43 P	12:21:51 P	
D01	Random Fact	matte			00:10	12:23:48 P	12:23:56 P	
D02	12n LA Finger Prints	Tammy	013	VO	00:25	12:23:59 P	12:24:06 P	
D03	12n Tel Aviv Cafe	Tammy		RDR	00:28	12:24:24 P	12:24:31 P	
D04	12n Two Shot	Tammy; Glenn			00:10	12:24:52 P	12:24:59 P	
D05	12n Entertainment	Glenn; Glenn	033	PKG	01:20	12:25:03 P	12:25:09 P	
D06	12n Bump Four	Glenn; Tammy	BUMP 4		00:22	12:26:23 P	12:26:29 P	
E00	--- B R E A K ---				02:05	12:26:39 P	12:26:51 P	
E01	Stocks				00:10	12:28:44 P	12:28:56 P	
E02	Weather/Traffic	Tammy; Glenn			00:20	12:28:54 P	12:29:06 P	
E03	12n Crazy Cars	Tammy	019	VO	00:20	12:29:14 P	12:29:26 P	
E04	Goodbye	Tammy; Glenn; Tammy			00:14	12:29:34 P	12:29:46 P	

FIG. 3.5.   Producer rundown.

away, Nashville's fame as a center of country music and the migration of many people from Tennessee to Georgia and Florida meant there would be people in the audience who would be interested in the story. The producer and the news anchor discussed the possibility of taking the live shot, and ultimately, it led the broadcast.

The producer was in an awkward position because both anchors were more experienced, but everyone handled the work relationship well. At one point, one of the anchors suggested a change in the item order, to facilitate camera shots. Later that anchor caught the producer's typographical error in a script.

The producer said she liked to have a reasonably firm rundown ready by 10 a.m. for the noon newscast. She relied on the news anchor for much of the writing, while an intern wrote the noon "teases," the short "stay-tuned" reminders that precede each commercial break. Another intern was asked to time a piece of video and make certain the scenes agreed or "conformed" with the anchor script. This was done because the feature was about automobiles and it would not have looked right have one auto on the screen while the anchor was talking about another vehicle.

Noon producers frequently have to work with whatever is left over from the previous day, plus feeds from the network and other features because there are usually fewer stories to cover in the morning, and most stations have to save their resources for the all important early- and late-evening broadcasts. Noon producers usually try to work the telephones (have someone make calls to police and fire agencies to pick up spot occurrences, which can be written to be read on camera by the anchor). Occasionally a major spot story will break overnight or early in the morning, such as a major accident during the morning rush hour, or the president will make a statement from the White House at 10 a.m. Then the noon producer's respiration increases with the rush of adrenaline that comes from having something new and interesting to get ready for the broadcast. In a small market, the noon producer can become very busy, cutting tape, writing, and continuing to update the rundown.

Channel One: Another Example

Channel One was an all-news cable channel in London, England that went out of business for lack of sponsors, but developed techniques that since have been copied by other news organizations. At the time of our visit, Channel One was a relatively new operation trying to capture viewers in an under-cabled city in competition with the local news departments of the British Broadcasting Corporation (BBC) and the independent commercial television stations.

The highly computerized, automated news operation at Channel One provided an innovative way of producing the news for television. Instead of producing one program rundown for a broadcast that would be aired at a specific time, the duty producer was filling in a constantly moving rundown (called a running-order in England), which reflected what was currently on the air, and what had not yet arrived, or was not edited for air. The work atmosphere was entirely different from a TV station because the producer had a deadline every minute.

In a typical hour, the producer had 23:51, 23 minutes, 51 seconds, to fill. There was some elasticity in the programming. Music beds and information about upcoming programming could be slipped in to make up for a segment that was running short.

In any "rolling" format, the assumption is that the viewing audience keeps changing, so it is acceptable to run stories more than once. However, producers like to have stories recut or altered, so the duty producer input instructions on the keyboard and sent them to editing. When the editing was done, the editor sent a note via computer that filled in a spot on the rolling running order. That told the producer the editing was done and the tape had been sent to the automated tape player to stand by for output.

A producer at Channel One relied heavily on the news desk and the video editors to get material ready before initial broadcast and to make changes when the content was being reused. The producer checked little filled-in color blocks on the computer running order to check that the work requested had been done.

HELPING REPORTERS

A producer's job resembles that of an orchestra conductor. The conductor coaches and chides until talented individuals work creatively and cooperatively to perform music. A producer aims for the highest quality output and, to get there, spends a great deal of time feeding creative ideas to people and keeping track of what sort of work reporters, writers, videographers, technicians, and video editors are doing.

Coaching is one of the tasks that falls on a producer's shoulders. A producer has to know how a story should be done, and then encourage or browbeat a reporter or videographer into doing the best work of which he or she is capable. The producer is expected to maintain the level of quality.

In larger newsrooms, reporters often find they start their day taking instructions from the assignment editor, and end the day taking instructions from a producer. The end-of-the-day phase is extremely important to a reporter. He or she has been out in the community all day, putting up with all the difficulties that accompany trying to gather information and shoot interviews for a story. Finally, the parts are coming together, and the reporter begins to focus on the product, which is the story.

The producer needs to define the task. For example, she might tell the reporter the story is slated for the first section, the ideal length is 1:20 (1 minute, 20 seconds), and it will follow a live feed from the network's affiliate news service. The most helpful information a producer can provide is to tell the reporter how the story fits into the broadcast. Will it be paired with another story? How much time has been allocated? Where is it positioned in the broadcast? Will the reporter be doing a live studio or newsroom introduction? Of course, the producer must be certain the reporter is given, or directed to, the latest relevant information from the wire services or other reporters. In short, a reporter needs to know how his or her piece is going to fit into the overall broadcast.

EDITING

A major weakness noted about television news in discussions at professional meetings and on the Internet is the lack of editing. By editing, I mean careful reading of the script for style, accuracy, grammar, and spelling. The three primary concerns are accuracy (libel prevention), grammar and word choice, and making certain the "piece" really tells the story. Here are examples of mistakes that should not occur:

- "... *less than* four people were involved." Does this mean 3.74 people, or does it mean somewhere between zero and three? The reporter meant to say *fewer than*.
- How many times have you heard a reporter say *cite* when paraphrasing a statement. People don't go around citing, unless they are law professors, or parking police. People *say* things.

Little mistakes make the reporter look and sound unprofessional or even stupid, and reflect poorly on the station. True, not everyone in the audience will catch the mistake, but enough people will recognize a wrong usage or sloppy statement to hurt a news department's reputation.

No writer is perfect. If you were to sit down with the writers on any major network news broadcast, you would hear tales about the things they wished they had not written! Editing improves communication and it improves performance. Editing also promotes *continuity,* meaning the logical thread of news items and *conformance,* meaning adhering to style rules that are applied by the news operation in order to use the same approach to language and writing for all the staff.

Some reporters are so resistant to having anyone look at their script that they find ways to make it impossible to see the script before the piece goes on the air. One common strategy is to wait to the last minute to finish the script. Another is to record the narration track in the field. Both of these hurt the reporter and the station.

Good management policy, and producers who are determined to keep quality, first can stop reporters from using these strategies to avoid editing. A skilled producer will have a backup story ready if it becomes necessary to cure the reporter who won't submit copy for editing by dropping the reporter's piece. Each time that reporter has story that doesn't get on air because it was not edited, he or she accumulates a negative mark on his or her work record.

The producer should discuss the video with the reporter, so that both understand what the piece ought to contain. The producer is the person who must conceptualize the broadcast and decide what video should be used.

Quality control requires that someone other than the reporter or writer review the finished product. If the producer can't get to it, someone should be designated to review every story before it goes on the air. This makes sense from the point of view of preventing lawsuits, as well as promoting quality writing and avoiding production errors. The bottom line: is the piece (script and video) clear and understandable? Do we gain information from it? Does the piece "tell the story"?

Some anchors check copy very carefully. This is good, the more backups the better. However, a producer can reduce tension in the newsroom by making certain the anchors get clean, approved copy. The newsroom gets stressful when the anchors find that they are saddled with copy that reads poorly or doesn't make sense. As the time approaches to go on the air, their commentary on the writing can be quite damaging to egos.

Occasionally you will hear a sweeping generalization that television news does not have editors. In small operations in which people have heavy workloads, editing can be limited. Sometimes the editing task is shared informally among the news director, anchors, and producers. Yet it is critical that editing be done in small newsrooms. This is where the majority of broadcast journalists begin their careers.

Some television news operations do have editors. WTVT in Tampa, Florida puts the weight of the editing on the producer, but assigns writers to each broadcast so that the producer is not bogged down writing on-camera stories.

CNN assigns copy editors to major broadcasts. A copy editor may not necessarily work on just one broadcast, but one is assigned in time to handle the copy flow leading up to air time. The three older networks, ABC, CBS, and NBC, all have people assigned to editing functions with each broadcast.

People do good work when they know they must. This is why it is so important for producers to set high standards for the participants in their broadcast.

PERFORMANCE

We dread admitting it, but the on-air staff in television has to be able to "act." A producer can help a reporter, and improve the broadcast, by giving the reporter input on performance. This includes voice quality and reading, the questions asked, eye contact, dress, movement, and blocking (positioning yourself and the people you interview). The contradiction in doing television reporting is that the reporter frequently has to do unnatural movements in order to appear natural. Walking is difficult on television, yet moving about slowly and smoothly lends style and interest and helps to tie together parts of stories. Reporters should not draw attention to their performance because the viewer loses focus on the point of the story.

Producers should not stare at monitors and complain about a reporter's mannerisms or distracting behavior out of the reporter's hearing. One of the producer's chores is to teach and improve the work of reporters and writers. It's difficult dealing with egos, but concerned, helpful, nonjudgmental advice will help a reporter to do a better job.

Producers both assist and train reporters in fact-gathering. If a producer realizes additional information is needed, he or she should bring it to the attention of the reporter or delegate someone else to follow up. The producer must then see that both sources exchange information or that it is put in the reporter's e-mail file in the computer system.

THE PRODUCERS DESK

FIG. 3.6. Weathercasters have one of the most difficult presentation tasks in live television. All the maps the weathercaster points to are added to the final picture in the control room. The weathercaster has to view the maps on monitor screens and position himself as if there were a map on the blue screen to which he is pointing. Producers and directors can be very helpful in assisting the on-air forecaster. Photo courtesy WCTV, Tallahassee, Florida.

Producers should talk with reporters as early as possible in the shift, and help plot the course of the story. Frequently a producer can suggest other sources, or a different approach. A producer, as one who is not involved, can see that a story is unbalanced or in need of another element, and therefore counsel the reporter to provide the necessary balance.

Part of a producer's responsibilities is to critique a reporter's work, including the weak aspects. This is where good people skills and diplomacy come in. No one likes to be criticized, yet everyone wants feedback. The art is to create an atmosphere in which criticism is helpful and positive, not denigrating.

HELPING CREWS IN THE FIELD

Producers assist crews in the field by having an overview of what is going on, as well as having access to material that may come in from other sources. The bottom line for a producer is to turn out a broadcast that is interesting, informative, and balanced. It's perfectly appropriate for a producer, either by speaking to the assignment editor or by talking with a reporter directly, to make suggestions, feed information, and check on progress.

Probably the most important service a producer provides to the newsgathering teams is making certain they are informed about breaking news or happenings which affect their story. During one of the author's observation visits, the Fox affiliate in Tampa, Florida, WTVT, reported on a very difficult story in which events were taking place in several locations. The story had begun the day before. It was about high school students in a suburban community who were said to have plotted to kill their parents. A father of one of the teens was found dead.

The next day the station had crews at a number of locations: the school the students attended, the residence where the father was found, the county jail, the county courthouse, and the county school board offices. All these places were covered to provide balance and a complete overview of a complicated and still emerging situation. One suspect was arrested at his grandmother's house in Mobile, Alabama. The producer and the satellite coordinator tried to obtain coverage tape from a Mobile station. One source that was discussed for a possible interview was a psychologist who might be able to discuss possible effects on teens of viewing satanic movies or visiting certain Internet sites. Complicating coverage was the problem that the estranged wife of the victim lived about 40 miles away in the Orlando area.

The point here is that the assignment desk and the producers had to keep exchanging information among the crews so that each knew what else was happening in regard to story details, structure, and content. The assignment desk was responsible for keeping in touch with the newsrooms of cooperating stations in Mobile and Orlando, and the Conus news bureau in Tallahassee but the evening producers had to coordinate all the information coming in locally and decide what they needed done for their broadcasts. Without proactive participation from producers the crews in the field would have been frustrated and the total coverage would have been ragged and confusing. Instead, crews were pulled off nonproductive assignments quickly, so they didn't sit around being bored, and everyone was given information on available video, as well as instructions how to make the different parts of the story fit together. This involved not repeating information contained in a prior segment of the report, and providing smooth transitions from reporter to reporter, by using specific "tosses," for example: "John Jones covered the arraignment at the Hillsborough County Courthouse." [Switch to Jones]

There is a trend toward turning microwave transmission vans and satellite newsgathering trucks into miniature bureaus by adding production equipment. Some stations include cellular telephone links for both voice and data in the trucks' equipment and supply reporters with laptop computers. Ideally, the laptop becomes an extension of the newsroom computer system.

Video can be edited on some laptops. Wire copy and messages can be forwarded to the reporter, and the reporter can submit scripts for approval before recording them, or reading them live. Requiring script approval not only helps to eliminate legal and language problems, it makes a small group of people, the producers, respon-

THE PRODUCERS DESK   47

sible for maintaining a consistent look and sound to stories in keeping with the "style" news broadcast the station strives to produce.

A word about bureaus: Many news organizations have staff stationed in remote locations. For example, a station may have a state capital bureau. Where two or three major cities make up the television market, it may be necessary to have bureaus in communities other than where the studios are located. Several cable news organizations cover metropolitan areas (greater Chicago), states (Ohio) or regions (New England), and have to have bureaus throughout their territory.

The newsroom computer system can be linked to these bureaus, so that wires may be read, scripts reviewed, other news broadcasts viewed and the archives used for research. Not only is this efficient, it helps the bureau personnel to feel they are a part of the organization, although they seldom visit the headquarters newsroom. Producers play an important role in creating a teamwork environment with staff members working in bureaus.

SCOPING OUT THE VIDEO

Television is about pictures. Television has become very graphic—using video and electronics to put many images on the screen. We know viewers watch TV more than they listen, so a producer has to be constantly seeking video to use to illustrate stories.

There are several ways we use video:

- Video over narration (Voice-over or VO)
- Video and sound on tape combined with narration (VO/SOT)
- A complex story involving more than one SOT insert plus illustrative video that may have "wild sound," background sound, on its audio track.

We can add an array of graphics to the video, including names and titles, still inserts such as lists or charts, freeze frames, picture rotation, page turns, boxes and dissolves.

A producer has to know how these graphic effects will enhance a story, and which ones can be included in the script using the newsroom computer system and which effects must be inserted at other stages in the production of a broadcast. It is important to balance the use of graphics. They should explain, illustrate, or make the story seamless. They should not draw undue attention to the graphic itself. (Television is about illusion, we don't want the audience to realize we have made an edit, or used a graphic. The audience member need not be aware that we put together bits and pieces to create a smooth, seamless story.)

Graphics and video should tell the story, move if forward, and most important, be truthful.

For example, character generator titles are important, we should identify people and places. But, we should not insert a CG that blocks important video, and we should not overuse CG inserts.

48   CHAPTER 3

At times television producers have fallen prey to the "MTV syndrome," videos full of fast cuts, bright colors, and dazzling effects. If viewers are watching the effects, we probably aren't getting the point of the story.

SOURCES

If you observe a television producer at work, you will probably wonder where all the video comes from. Here are some sources:

- Video the news organization's videographers shoot.
- Selected video from network and local programs. (An excerpt from a public affairs program.)
- The networks' affiliates exchange. ABC, CBS, CNN, NBC and Fox provide feeds of some of their surplus video, plus a small amount of original work, and stories submitted to the network by affiliates as part of an exchange agreement.
- CNN, APTV, Reuters—Contract video suppliers.
    CNN sells video.
    APTV is the video news service of the Associated Press. It sells video.
    Reuters is another commercial news video service. It is similar to the Associated Press
- Public relations video stories supplied in behalf of companies, nonprofit organizations, or causes.
- State, or regional news exchanges, such as the Florida News Network, that has one member station in each major Florida market city.
- Company bureaus—major chain broadcasters maintain bureaus, especially in Washington, DC.
- Earlier broadcasts on the producer's station.
- Video shot by the public (usually used for breaking news).

A lot of video flows into a station's recording equipment. There are several ways in which a producer becomes aware of the video available in house. The network affiliate services and the paid suppliers provide shot lists and scripts through data links (mainly e-mail) or a wire service. The producer can call up these lists on a terminal. Producers can view lists that appear on video screens when feeds are underway. Many services provide audio alerts regarding upcoming video feeds.

Generally one or more of the major services such as CNN or an affiliates service can be viewed on monitors in the newsroom while the feed is coming in. Stations either record the feeds on videotape or on computer servers.

Some advanced newsroom computer workstations can show moving video on the computer screen providing the video is stored in a digital computer server. Most "browse" systems feed low-resolution video to workstations. The video consists of a sampling of frames pulled from the source video. This is enough for a producer to

FIG. 3.7. A laptop computer (foreground) and a flat screen monitor (center) show how a video image (the fire shown on the studio monitor on the right of this picture) can be viewed on a producer's terminal, along with the relevant script. Writers can import video and either edit it or prepare an "edit decision list" for a video editor, as well as write the copy to accompany the video. © 2004 Avid Technology, Inc. All rights reserved. Avid is a registered trademark or trademark of Avid Technology, Inc., in the United States and/or other countries. Photo is provided courtesy of Avid Technology, Inc.

judge the content of a story. Getting high-resolution (real time) video at work stations is dependent on major upgrades to computer equipment.

A producer will narrow down the choices, then assign someone to look at the video that might be usable. At CNN, the inventory of video is enormous, but a producer can use a terminal to request a specific piece of video, which is stored on a video server. In a few seconds, the video can be viewed at the workstation, having been sent over a computer network from the server.

CONCLUSION

In this chapter, I have discussed the relationships between producers and the many sources of stories, including local crews, bureaus, and news services. In the next chapter, I focus on the process of weaving all the information into a structure that allows us to create a television news broadcast.

4
Gathering Up the Bits and Pieces

Observe the typical television news producer at work and you will get two impressions: first, the producer spends a lot of time working on the computer, and second, it looks as if there's an awful jumble of partly done projects that need to be finished in time for the news.

The reason producers spend a lot of time with their keyboard and mouse is that they look at wire copy, check out available video, read scripts, read messages, do research, and then, as parts of the broadcast come together, enter the information into the rundown, which is constantly being changed.

Producing is a balancing act. A producer usually has to live with the uncertainty of having a lot going on, and little coming to fruition until the hour before broadcast time. Unless stories have been completed earlier in the day, reporters generally check in late because they are still gathering information and assembling their stories. As they begin to write, changes occur, either because the needed video isn't available, or a late phone call changes the focus of the story, or simply because the reporter or writer finds a better way to tell the story once they focus on writing.

All producers strive to have as many elements firmed up as possible early in the day. If there is something on a feed that will fit into the broadcast, a producer will arrange to have it pulled out of the inventory of feeds, and either write an anchor lead-in, or assign it to be written. If the format calls for ending with a feature perhaps an appropriate piece of video can been found among the feeds or shot locally early in the day. Many producers will write two or three brief on-camera or voice-over items that can be used as fillers, if a scheduled item doesn't come in on time.

There are many bits and pieces that have to be listed and checked. These include graphics, such as CGs, still stores, and freeze frames. Most producers try to make early decisions on any graphics that need to be created by an artist because the art or graphics department needs time to do the work. A new producer should spend some time with the graphics staff to learn what facilities they have, the type of graphics they can produce, and what kind of timelines are needed to produce certain types of graphics.

GATHERING BITS AND PIECES   51

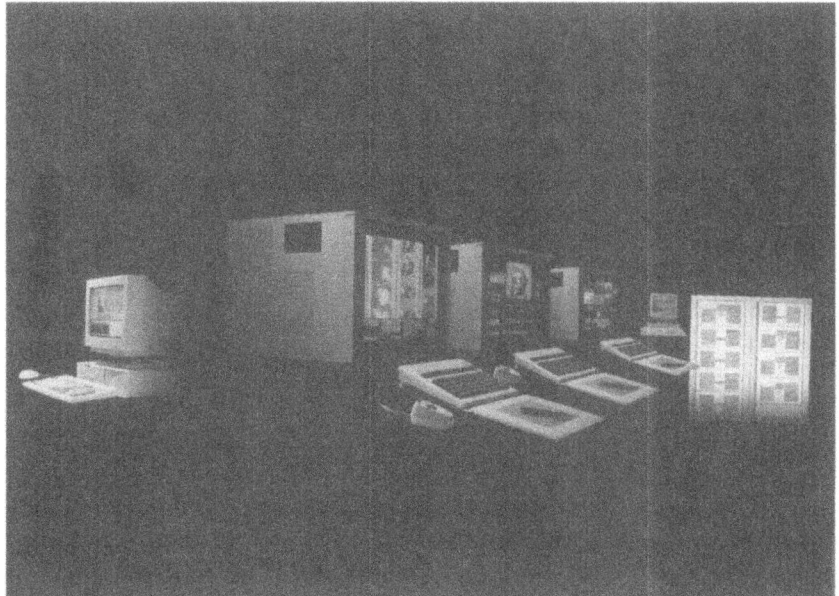

FIG. 4.1. Producers should become acquainted with the capabilities of various graphic devices, such as the Quantel Editbox. Courtesy Quantel.

Video that needs to be taken from earlier stories is also ordered early so that it can be pulled out by the editing staff and the accompanying script written.

Larger news organizations assign specific staff to certain detail work. Production assistants frequently check and assemble information about character generator titles and tapes needing to be delivered and checked off on the rundown. Many stations use associate producers as in-house producers for live feeds. This takes a lot of last minute detail work off the list of tasks the producer has to accomplish.

Some operations have a news operations manager who takes charge of the technical side of remote broadcasts, so that the producers don't have to be involved in the technical details of setting up live coverage.

THE ALMOST FINAL RUNDOWN AND SCRIPT

Typically the newsroom computer system has rundown check and reminder systems. Each blank on the format on the screen must be completed before an item listed for the broadcast is cleared for air. Some computer systems use color cues for checking off "script done," "read," and "approved." Producing used to require keeping a lot of notes and lists on the desk, but the newsroom computer has made it easier to organize information so a producer can tell what is missing. Some computer programs permit members of the production staff to pull out the specific information as they need it, such as character generator screens, others simply include this information in the overall rundown.

Copies of the rundown and script are printed because so-called "hard copy" is more convenient for some production staff members to use, and many anchors like to have a backup hard copy of the script on their desks. Many other people involved in the production of the broadcast work from computer screens. The director, producer, and CG operator are likely to use screens. In many news organizations, the anchors have the script on computers that are built into their studio desks.

One thing that makes television exciting is that technology makes it possible to cover late-breaking stories and get them in a news broadcast. As much as possible, producers try to set up live feeds ahead of time, so that probable difficulties can be anticipated, and dealt with. But, if a story breaks right before broadcast time, or even while the broadcast is on the air, the station may be able to move a microwave or satellite truck into place, and do live coverage. This means no script, and it means retiming the news program as it is being aired.

The rundown isn't finished, in many situations, until the broadcast is over.

LIVING WITH LIVE SHOTS

We hear a lot about doing "live shots" during television news programs. How are they done?

Microwave is a transmission technology that sends an audio/video signal from a mobile unit to a receiver located no more than 30 to 40 miles from the mobile unit. The microwave signal travels in a straight line from a mast mounted on a van, truck, or sport utility vehicle to a receiver, which is frequently mounted on the TV station's transmission tower. The signal is then fed to the master control area, either by microwave or by cable. Microwave transmission (frequently called *ENG* for electronic news gathering) requires a line-of-sight pathway to the receiver.

Satellite newsgathering requires a larger vehicle to support the mobile uplink antenna and carry the transmitters and one or two electrical generators. The signal originating from the satellite news vehicle (SNV) is transmitted to an antenna on a *transponder* (which is like a "channel" on a TV receiver) on in a fixed orbit, 22,300 miles above the equator. The satellite returns the signal to earth where it is received on a fixed antenna, called an *earth station*. Some broadcasters have earth station equipment on their sites, but the handling of the transmission is done through companies that own the satellites or maintain clusters of earth stations, which are sometimes called *spaceports* or *teleports*. These companies lease out time on their "occasional use" transponders for news feeds. They also provide two-way communications between the newsroom and the mobile truck.

Some satellites are positioned to cover most of the U.S. Generally satellite technology is best used beyond the range of microwave, where it would be too expensive to lease a video line. Some SNVs carry a second antenna so that they can be used for microwave coverage when the unit is within about 40 miles of the station, making the SNV more cost-effective.

FIG. 4.2. A typical Satellite News Vehicle (SNV), which is a portable satellite unlink/downlink mounted on a heavy truck chassis. The transmit/receive dish is folded inward so that it rests on the unit's roof. This type of vehicle can transmit live television video and audio over long distances and is fully self-sufficient for use in remote areas. Photo courtesy of Frontline Communications, Clearwater, Florida.

Satellite and ENG vehicles are usually equipped with cables, cameras, and camera controls (besides the portable camera), and basic switching and editing equipment, and lights adequate for producing a live news cut-in. Some are equipped with special voice communication circuits, others rely on cellular telephone circuits to keep in touch with the newsroom.

A field producer may be sent along on major stories, but in most instances, the reporter and truck operator handle production details with the station. There has been a small trend toward trying to hire multiskilled personnel to operate the live trucks. Typically a microwave truck operator is also a videographer and editor. Operators of SNVs have tended to be engineers because the equipment frequently requires service or repair in the field. Special driver licenses are also required for some SNVs. A trend has arisen toward using more compact ENG and SNV units and requiring, for instance, a sports reporter to also know how to operate the mobile van.

Working on a live shot requires special attention from producers. A couple of hints garnered from experienced producers: (1) Know something about the story before the crew leaves the studio. A worst-case backup is to write a very general (i.e., *generic*) lead-in; (2) Read your introduction and (if there is one) lock-out to the reporter to see if it coordinates with what the reporter plans to say; (3) Make certain the reporter has supplied you with the supers for the report; (4) Pay close attention to the background when the picture comes up, and recommend a change if it doesn't look right; (5) Train crews to report in as early as possible, in fact, you should carry on a dialogue with live crews during the day, and discuss how to tell the story.

PRODUCTION CONTROL

The actual control and decision-making process involved in transmitting a news broadcast live is usually overseen by a director. The director is responsible for seeing that all the elements of a news broadcast are inserted properly on the air. The director controls camera shots, starting tape or disk pieces, inserting graphics, audio, and lighting. The director usually sits down with the producer about an hour before the news program goes on the air and talks over what is desired. The director is responsible for the aesthetic element of the broadcast. Automation makes it unnecessary for the director to have to coordinate with a dozen specialized technicians, but the director still determines the moment when a function is executed, usually by the technical director, who is sitting in front of a large video console equipped with buttons and levers that start and stop equipment, put camera shots on the air, and cause various graphic effects to occur. Usually the control room will also be staffed by a video operator, an audio operator and a character generator operator. Stations that transmit news stories on tape usually require one or two tape deck operators. In most cases, the producer sits close by, watching the rundown on a computer terminal and conferring with the director. Larger broadcast organizations may have several other people in the control room, including associate producers who handle getting live remotes ready to go on the air. The studio crew may include camera operators and a floor manager or floor director who communicates with the talent. Automation technology is gradually cutting down on individual camera operators in favor of having one technician control all studio cameras from a special console. Some facilities require an operator to control the prompting device.

PRODUCING THE NEWS, A LOOK AT TWO FACILITIES

WTVT

WTVT Television is the Fox affiliate in Tampa, Florida, which is in the 11-20 tier of markets. The station, on channel 13, was a CBS affiliate for many years and had a built-in reputation for excellence in news coverage. New owners (FOX stations) converted it to a FOX affiliate, but because it is owned by the parent network, the station is regarded as a showpiece and a source of support for the national FOX news organization. The station does early morning news, a noontime hour, 5 p.m. hour, 6 p.m. hour, and 10 p.m. hour.

The visit to WTVT started with the morning meeting, a tradition in most television newsrooms. The meeting was attended by the news director plus 10 staff members. The general manager dropped in for a while.

GATHERING BITS AND PIECES

News Director: Do we broadcast this morning's 11 a.m. press conference at the White House, featuring President Bill Clinton and British Prime Minister Tony Blair? The consensus is yes. A producer is assigned because the station is taking a clean feed (no commentary from a network correspondent), so they would have to use a local anchor to introduce and close the broadcast.

General manager and news director agree—the station will take some, but might not take all of the feed if the press questioning doesn't justify further coverage. The subject is supposed to be a crisis in Iraq—should the UN bomb Iraq to force compliance with the UN mandate to destroy "weapons of mass destruction"? It is expected to quickly descend into questions about President Clinton's alleged conduct with a White House intern, Monica Lewinsky. (Producers and other midlevel executives attending the meeting had read the *New York Times,* the *Tampa Tribune,* and the *St. Petersburg Times.*)

News Director: What's available? A producer reports the station's Consumer Lawyer is nearly ready with a piece on "Dating Services, what to look for, how much to pay."

It is assigned to the 5 p.m. newscast.

Consumer Solutions (feature title) has "What to do with HMO (health maintenance organization) paperwork?" ready. It is assigned to 6 p.m. newscast.

The general manager comes in, and the news director briefs him on the Clinton live news conference. The general manager agrees it should be carried although it doesn't appear to be very newsworthy. Graphics and producer assignments are made. (At the point the meeting becomes more free-flowing with the news director and assignment manager and senior producers injecting comments or introducing topics.)

The big story: Lakeland—Students plot to kill parents, one student does kill a parent and is picked up in Mobile, Alabama at his grandmother's home. This was a breaking story yesterday, and is already staffed this morning—what happens today?

Counselors will be talking to students at the high school, two of the youths will make first appearances in court.

Any background on the man killed? Yes, he was a physical education teacher until 1986. He may have worked for the Internal Revenue Service at one time.

The Orlando CONUS affiliate will cover his estranged wife.

Ideas brought up—find the woman in California who one suspect communicated with via Internet chats. See if Web sites can be tracked.

Comment: An effort was made last night, but there were technical problems with the Internet service. (Two crews are assigned.)
Question: Where do kids get these ideas?

Response:	Ideas for the satanic actions of these students may have come from a movie.
News Director:	Try to get other parents who supposedly were on the hit list. Talk to a local psychologist about movie influence angle. (The station has a psychologist who the station regularly interviews.)
Comment:	The murder suspect reportedly would stay on the computer for hours.
Producer:	How do kids think like this?
Question:	Who could do a sidebar? (i.e., a supplemental feature story).

A discussion of other stories continues:

Holocaust Museum—the package needs a fix—it's getting outdated. (Agreement to fix production problem and play it soon.)

Florida State Fair near Tampa—Was underplayed yesterday on opening day.

News Director comments: Fair stuff was available but it was not well packaged by producers.

Gasparilla Festival (annual pageant): A reporter will do this for 5 and 6. There is discussion of people staking out viewing spots already for tomorrow afternoon's parade. (A producer commented that people stake out places well ahead of time, even set up portable toilets.)

"I've never seen anything like this," says one participant.

Decisions—Fair—*Air 13* (leased helicopter) will be sent to videotape—be sure to get crowd shots. (Rain had reduced the opening day crowds yesterday.)

Reporter:	The tax story I am working on will be done this morning, and I will then go to fair. It's the "Fair Tax" (name of tax group) story.
News Director:	Hold it for 10 p.m. sometime next week.

Washington (Fox) will handle feed of President.

Story on swarming termites, caused by unusually wet and warm weather. (News Director likes the story.)

The smart bomb story can be rerun at noon and 5.

Gasparilla can be covered at noon and 5 also.

Yoko Ono Art feature? Discussion of its status. Someone reports that the senior reporter called in sick, but he is needed to voice the feature. The news director points out it is ratings month and the reporter needs to be heard. (The ratings period started the day before.)

"Get sound at school in Lakeland. Send Rosa (reporter) to first appearances of Lakeland youths. Goff will do noon live shot at Lakeland."

The News Director says he liked the Police laser gun story yesterday.

The general manager talks about the February sweeps ratings period—Thursday night (the last night) is traditionally weak for Fox, but *The Nancy Kerrigan Show* on Fox boosted ratings significantly.

GATHERING BITS AND PIECES 57

"What is the gun series about?"

"An antigun group released a study."

More discussion of termites—termite exterminators are going nuts because of heavy rains in the Duneden area

One producer remembers the senior reporter did a termite story—he might be a source (producer told to check the system's archives).

(Phone call—the CONUS capital bureau in Tallahassee joins the meeting.) The bureau chief says the Orlando affiliate will do a follow-up on finding the mother of a baby abandoned at Disney World. The mother was located in the Philippines, she will be extradited to the U.S. to stand trial.

(The news director tells the CONUS bureau chief he should send the bureau reporter to the capitol to shake hands and generally prepare for coverage of legislature, which convenes in March.)

Discussion of impending executions—The CONUS bureau chief reports that the next execution is scheduled for late February. A second execution is scheduled at 9 a.m. February 25th. The news director thanks the CONUS bureau chief, after reminding him to watch the Orlando affiliate for a feed on the divorced mom of the Lakeland teenager who is accused of killing his parent.

Assignment manager says that leaves us with one floating reporter.

News Director: Do the story on kids making money by scanning currency on a computer? Shoot video for noon on Gasparilla and Fair. (The Senior sports reporter calls in ...)

More talk about kids printing cash with a computer. The news director says not to show people how to do it.

A call from the assignment desk: A body has been found south of Manatee—it is believed to be that of a missing boater—a fishing boat and a recreational boat had collided, two people are missing. A videographer is on the way.

News Director: Are we running anything from the Nancy Kerrigan special last night?

Discussion, some grumbling because it was an entertainment program, they finally agree to run a short piece, primarily video.

Four people are working on the Lakeland murder—a cameraman has been assigned to the helicopter, which has its own built-in camera, too.

The group then talks about Saturday coverage. The general manager comments that the Gasparilla Festival starts in the afternoon Saturday. He reminds the producers to pay attention to traffic problems.

The general manager then says he has 120 hours of helicopter time budgeted before the end of the fiscal year, so use some of it. (The meeting lasted 35 minutes.)

Following the Morning Meeting, we observe the 5 p.m. producer. He graduated from Colorado State University and worked in radio news and did some disk jockey work for 2 years. Then he moved to WINK-TV in Ft. Myers, Florida for 2 years. From there he moved to WTVT and has been at the station for 5 years. Early in his WTVT tenure, he did some assignment desk duty.

Producers work in desk areas called *producer pods*. The team includes two to three writers for each hour show, but they are shared. Producers usually write the teases. They do this early to get it out of the way. Following the 2 p.m. editorial meeting the writers start writing for the 5 p.m. Writers at this station are called associate producers, many become producers.

Some anchors sit next to the producer in the pod and try to sit in on the 2 p.m. meeting. We are told some anchors write "a little." They also have offices along the newsroom wall.

Feeds can be monitored at the producer's desk. The producer has a switch to select video channels to monitor, including Fox, CNN, and CONUS national or local feeds from the field. The main copy sources are the AP and Reuters.

The 5 p.m. producer may use four to six daytime crews. The producer tries to use at least three reporters live, two in the first half hour and one in the second half hour, plus packaged reports such as consumer items.

The station has six ENG trucks and one SNV. WTVT leases a helicopter with two mounted cameras, nose and tail, and frequently puts a videographer aboard. A new gyro stabilizer system is being installed at cost of $175,000. The pilot can and does voice news, and does a traffic insert in the 5 p.m. hour.

The weekday news hole at 5 p.m. is about 12 minutes per half hour. There is some weather and sports in the 5 p.m. but not much sports because the 5 p.m. gets female demographics in the ratings and studies of ratings across the country indicate diminished female viewing when sports reports are running. Usually the sports reports consist of scores and updates on sports of the day and a package.

The newsroom computer system is an early product from BASYS and still has old "dumb" terminals wired to a minicomputer rather than personal computers. The Fox company has bought the first generation of AvidNews, and a windows-based AvidNews system is scheduled to be installed at WTVT in December. (Avid Technologies bought one of the pioneer systems, BASYS, and redesigned it and renamed the product AvidNews.)

The 5 p.m. producer is the chief operator of system. He controls allocation of passwords and troubleshoots when software problems arise. He said he got to be the chief operator because he was interested in computers. He had not trained at a BASYS school.

A "reality check" meeting takes place in the noon hour, but not always exactly at 12 p.m. Participants include the 5 p.m. and 6 p.m. producers and other involved people including the assignment manager. At 2 p.m. another full fledged meeting is held for the 5 p.m., 6 p.m., and 10 p.m. producers and their support personnel. The news director usually attends this meeting. After it adjourns the nightside staff has a planning meeting.

(We take a break to talk to the Director of Engineering who says the original BASYS newsroom computer system was installed in August, 1988. The station has bought all the software revisions so the system is relatively up-to-date from a software standpoint. The CPUs are three 486-66s which are 3½ to 4 years old. The system could run NetStation software on personal computers, but the previous owner of the station chose to stay with dumb terminals.

Fox is going to AvidNews. The Information Systems department will take over control of system from engineering. The current system has 50 terminals (seats), and 72 ports but needs more. The new system will have about 80 seats and 20 devices because the current staff is much larger than when station was a CBS affiliate.

The assignment desk has an Internet PC for research and Dow-Jones business resources. The newsroom currently has BASYS Archives I and II software. The new system will network to BASYS Archives II. All current editorial functions will be preserved, plus producers will be able to preview video and do editing decision lists for clips and feeds. Actual video editing will be done in edit suites to assure audio/video conformity. The director of engineering does not like the idea of editing video at a producer's or writer's desk.

Automation software will include a CG interface, prompting, and closed captioning, but not automated cameras. News is shot on beta-format tape and manually played out on tape decks.

WTVT had introduced new digital nonlinear video editing for promotions. The engineering director doesn't want the newsroom system to be too complex because

FIG. 4.3. A mini-DV (digital video) camcorder. It weighs 2.4 pounds and delivers high-quality professional video. This model offers infrared nighttime recording for shooting investigative stories at night when lights are not feasible. Photo courtesy of Panasonic Broadcast and Television Systems Co.

it must be user friendly. He was trained at an advanced BASYS school. He says training is easier now because almost everyone in the newsroom has a PC at home. The director of engineering says he will have all floppy drives on the new equipment disabled to prevent people from introducing viruses by bringing disks into the newsroom.

At 12:35 p.m., the noon meeting begins at the producer pod with the assignment manager, 5 p.m. producer, and 6 p.m. producer attending.

What do they have? The Lakeland murder—a package and the suspects' first appearance in court.

The 5 p.m. producer says his lead looks like President Clinton.

The 6 p.m. producer says her lead is the Lakeland murder. (While she is talking, the 5 p.m. producer is debriefing a reporter who just walked in.)

The 6 p.m. producer says: "My dream is to have a meeting without interruptions."

They talk about a missing child story. A picture of the child is going to be put on a trucking company's vehicles. The follow-up story is called "Sabrina."

Termites—everyone's lukewarm. The 5 p.m. producer takes the Holocaust story and "Sabrina."

The assignment manager suggests putting termites in the 5:30 p.m. to 6 p.m. segment as a live report.

The 6 p.m. producer says she will lead at 6:30 p.m. with Sabrina, the lost child.

Gasparilla Festival remote—up for both 5 p.m. and 6 p.m. The story should be tips on how to see the parade and deal with traffic.

Fair tax movement—the 5 p.m. is full, can't handle—6 p.m. is full with the State Fair and Gasparilla.

The 5 p.m. producer asks: "do we have b-roll (just pictures) of the Fair? The Assignment Editor says "yes."

The 6 p.m. producer says "hold the fair tax story for next week."

Kids make cash on computers—the 6 p.m. takes it.

Smart bomb—will tease at 6 p.m. and run at 10 p.m.

The Clinton press conference will run in both shows.

The Assignment Editor says voice-overs are available on the body found and a

Greek festival in Manatee. The 6 p.m. producer takes the festival to run with the State Fair. Question—what about Fair traffic? We need *Air 13* (helicopter). The assignment editor says its OK for 5 p.m. and 6 p.m. The 6 p.m. producer says she won't take the chopper after all due to rain and darkness—a big rain storm is moving in.

The assignment editor says the sheriff's department does "shoot, don't shoot" demonstrations for the public at the Fair. It's a demonstration of what deputies practice on the firing range. The producers are lukewarm—they say save it for 10 p.m. It's obvious the assignment editor would like to "sell" this one to promote good relations with the sheriff's department.

The assignment editor says he has a "light crime and grime" report, with very little video.

(During the meeting a senior producer joins the group along with a representative of the assignment planning desk.)

GATHERING BITS AND PIECES   61

The producers are concerned if the predicted big rainstorm will curb helicopter live shots. Someone says rain is predicted for this evening but should move out by tomorrow morning. The 5 p.m. producer says the chopper pilot will fly in rain and wind if visibility is not a problem.

The 5 p.m. producer is using a CNN piece with CNN's White House correspondent on what the White house will do about Iraq deeper into the show. (The meeting breaks up and the 6 p.m. producer orders lunch.)

The producer's rundown on the screen has a blank for approvals. It shows items ready and printed but doesn't always reveal changes. The time category is backtime. The reading time for anchors is calculated at two seconds per line of copy.

The 5 p.m. producer says he builds a pad into the newscast and pads his rundown times, plus he has short voice over items to use or delete for timing purposes.

Our attention is diverted to a bulletin visual on one of the network monitors. The producer turns up the CNN audio channel.

CNN Breaking News—interrupts CNN cable on a newsroom monitor—two F-18 aircraft collided in flight in the Persian Gulf.

The producer is informed video will be available of Lakeland suspect's Grandmother's house in Mobile and old video of the suspect will be sent by Mobile station in trade for live cut-in about the Lakeland killing.

TWO P.M. MEETING

The participants are the news director, the planning editor, the 5 p.m., 6 p.m., and 10 p.m. producers, and some of the nightside staff.

News Director: Says the story about the Lakeland murder—three teens charged with murder—made the AP wire with credit to WTVT for first reporting it to the AP.

The 5 p.m. Producer: New—Marine pilots rescued from the Gulf mid-air collision (one later died). They talk about getting someone from nightside to monitor the satellite center for late pieces or video. Discussion on the story. This is a military town (MacDill Air Force Base in Tampa houses the military headquarters responsible for the Mid-East region plus the area has many military retirees). The news director says people are frightened by the threat of war. Nightside negotiates out of providing a staffer for the satellite center, dayside provides.

News Director: What's new on Clinton? [He is told Special Prosecutor Kenneth Starr is complaining about leaks. The 5 and 6 producers say they will use CNN coverage. Some of Clinton at the morning news conference will be used.]

Lakeland murder—two youths were arraigned today, the third youth is being returned from Mobile, Alabama tonight. There are good pictures in the noon broadcast that can be used.

News Director: Check a fact: Were the kids charged as adults? One of the reporters on the story comes in and explains that he was told they were charged as adults by a state attorney, but he will check further.

Brief discussion of:
Body found.
Disney mom—she was supposedly identified through DNA of baby. The news director says let's get this DNA detective work explained.
State Fair—B roll—likely to be raining at 5 p.m. so we may not be using the helicopter.
Gasparilla preparations.
Iraq.
Teacher who had sex with a minor student (after conviction on similar charge) given 7½ years in prison.
Hutchins—suicide.
Mercury studies in Everglades—Mercury is coming from Europe across the Atlantic Ocean.
Balloonist is rescued.
The news director says one block is too short. The 5 p.m. producer points out the first block is too long. They make minor adjustments.
Sports.
Live report on termite problem from a residence.
Irvin's response to Reverend Lyons story—a local story.
The producer suggests switching the order of two items, the news director says leave them as is.
Holocaust story—has a bad edit—needs to be fixed. The news director says have someone do it soon.
Excerpt from network Nancy Kerrigan show night before with graphic to show highest ever ratings (this was suggested by general manager, some grumbling among producers, but in end they planned to do it on 5 p.m.).
Someone asked—why is it running? Answer: The general manager said to do it.
Weather.
Drug story.
Problem with Gasparilla Festival guns being too loud.
Columbia/HCA (for-profit hospital chain under federal investigation) may report a loss of one billion dollars.
Consumer lawyer feature.
Kicker—Gasparilla history.

The 6 p.m
Producer: Lead with the Lakeland murder—we have video of the third suspect.

(The Mobile, Alabama video is being driven to New Orleans where it will be fed on a fiber optic circuit to Tampa.)

GATHERING BITS AND PIECES 63

May open on great sound.
Sidebar—about the reaction of teens at the high school in Lakeland.
The news director suggests using a complex graphic—a triple box with three venues.
Body found.
Sabrina—lost child posters on trucks.
News director says add a live tease for Gasparilla.
Weather
Music star died
Bible class tape from CONUS Ft. Myers affiliate.
Kid counterfeiters—a local reporter went to the computer lab. News Director says, let's make sure it is a good story.

News Director:	What should we take out of the 5 p.m. show? (It is running long.)
The 6 p.m. Producer:	What is the status of *Air 13*? (She is concerned about the rain and darkness. This triggers a brief production discussion about using more light on night remotes.)

6:30—lead—Clinton crisis.
Missile test.
The news director asks about another teaser.
News director then asks, "How heavy is the show?"
The producer says, "2½ minutes over."
Teacher sex sentence.
Roy Roemer affair.
Reagan 87.
Stocks
Health maintenance organization story.
Kicker—Black History month feature.
Comment—kid counterfeiters could go tonight.
No. "We have depth!"
Then there is a brief discussion about WTVT letting stories run longer to permit them to have more detail (depth) than opposition.

Producer—discussion about over-runs by talent—the news director says he will meet with talent next week.

NIGHTSIDE : Planning Editor:

We owe the Mobile station a live shot at 7 p.m. in trade for tape of Lakeland suspect.
Lakeland murder—sent someone to Polk county.
New items—
Devil Rays—sports franchise.
Gasparilla get ready story.
On Mobile at 7 p.m.—have Rosa do the live shot.
That leaves two reporters.

The news director says have Jennifer work on the feature for Monday.

The Lakeland suspect has not left Mobile, may leave at 5 p.m.

Discussion: A pharmacist says he can document illegal actions by a pharmacy company. (Authorities have accused a company of fraudulent billing practices on prescriptions.) Discussion by news director and others about the reliability of the source. The news director says do it, cautiously.

Question: "Who is covering the airport for the return of the Lakeland suspect from Mobile?"

The assignment desk reminds the group about two school attacks in Brandon, one student-on-student, the other student-on-teacher.

An Editor: The pharmacist worries me.
News Director: Check with legal.
News Director: Are we done? (45 minute meeting)

Then he conducts a short discussion about the Marine aircraft midair crash story and a piece involving Eglin Air Force Base on the Florida panhandle.

There's one day in the life of a large-market television news department.

KNTV

The next station visit takes us to KTNV-TV in sixty-first market, Las Vegas, Nevada. The station is owned by Journal Communications, Inc., owner of WTMJ-TV in Milwaukee. Journal Communications owns television and radio stations and other communication industry properties.

KTNV is the test site for the latest version of the NewStar II newsroom computer system. Software companies frequently work out agreements with two or three customers to be "beta sites," test sites for new or updated software. KTNV agreed to test version 8 of the NewStar software.

KNTV installed the NewStar for Windows® software. The software features three work areas on a single screen. The producers usually put the rundown on the left, from top to bottom of the screen. A script that is being worked on can go on the upper right, and a list of other scripts in the rundown can go on the lower right. The windows can be used for other purposes according to the needs of the person working on a terminal.

The software has a drag-and-drop feature for changes in rundown, which means the producer can use the computer's mouse to move items on the monitor screen and execute changes. The NewStar software includes a Rolodex feature with staff and contact telephone numbers. It also has a "chat" function, which permits any NewStar user to send messages. This feature is most useful for stations that have bureaus or branch newsrooms.

GATHERING BITS AND PIECES

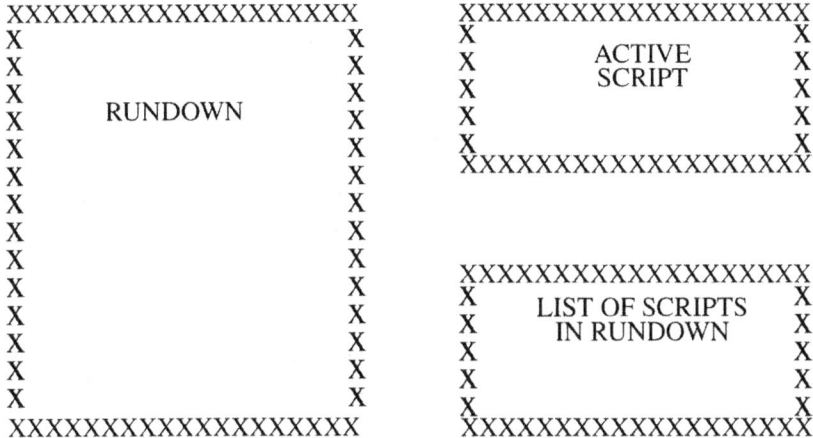

KTNV is an ABC affiliate on channel 13. The station presents local evening news from 5 to 5:30 p.m., then carries the *ABC Evening News* from 5:30 to 6 p.m., followed by two 30-minute local news broadcasts, 6 to 6:30 p.m. and 6:30 to 7 p.m. After the 6:30 to 7 p.m. broadcast, KTNV goes into prime time access at with the syndicated program, *Home Improvement*.

We observed the producer of the 6:30 to 7 p.m. newscast. The 6:30 producer comes to work at 10:30 a.m. and goes off at 7 p.m. As a result, he misses the 9 a.m. morning meeting where the day's lineup is sketched out and stories are assigned to specific broadcasts, and so he does not have direct input into a lot of the day's story lineup. Producers write stories if no reporter is assigned. These are usually short on-camera or voice-over tape items.

The producer graduated from Northwestern University in journalism and worked in TV news in Columbia, Missouri before moving to Las Vegas.

The 6:30 to 7 p.m. news program was inaugurated a year ago, and gets a 4 rating and an 8 share against the ever-popular syndicated program *Jeopardy* on a competing channel.

The 6:30 producer tries for different leads, although there can be some overlap with the two earlier local broadcasts. On the rundown, the 6 p.m. broadcast numbers its pieces with numbers starting at 100, whereas the 6:30 p.m. uses a letter code for each block.

Producers work in small carrels, which have low walls so they can talk to each other. Reporters can come by and talk collectively with the producers. The news director's office is a few feet away. The assignment desk area is close by, an assignment editor could attract attention by speaking loudly.

The day we visited was a very slow Friday. Just after we arrived the assignment desk messaged producers and others to say explosives had been discovered in a car towed to a police impound lot.

The 6:30 p.m. broadcast had only one or two local packages lined up. One would be the developing story about dynamite being found in the trunk of an abandoned car that had been towed to a storage lot from an apartment complex parking lot.

At 2 p.m. a breaking story develops. Earlier, a firm handling hazardous waste for Clark County had been caught burying waste materials. A clean up had been ordered and the firm had filed various protests. Today the company says it has decided to call it quits in Clark County, leaving only one firm to bid for the county hazardous waste disposal contract. The departing company is supposed to fax its official statement at 3:30 this afternoon.

The producers decide to lead with this development at 5 p.m. and again at 6:30 p.m. The producers and the managing editor meet informally in the middle of the newsroom to talk about the waste company closing. One producer remarks that there is B-roll (previously shot tape of the company's storage facility) in the archives. They discuss sending a live truck to the company's offices.

The "news hole" (time for actual news items) at 6:30 p.m. is about 12 minutes. Items being considered for the 6:30 p.m. news broadcast include:

- U.S. Medical leaving town (waste),
- Dynamite found in car, and
- Prisoner shot escaping in the Reno, Nevada area—he was shot and killed by a corrections officer. He was convicted of a highly publicized murder in Las Vegas, which is why KTNV is interested in the story.

FIG. 4.4. WTSP, St. Petersburg, Florida. Gannett-owned CBS affiliate has several Frontline ENGs and a Frontline full-size SNV. This van is a typical ENG van with a 42-foot mast, 2 Ghz Microwave Transmit System, and Full Beta Editing.

GATHERING BITS AND PIECES

The producer says he tries to include the most important national story, and some national/international briefs in his broadcast because people seldom watch 2 hours straight of TV news.

There is heavy reliance on stories that come into the station on satellite feeds. KTNV receives feeds from ABC's NewsOne and CNN. The producer can see scripts for both services. ABC provides on-line video streaming showing the stories on the feed in low resolution on the producer's workstation screen. NewsOne has a browser feature that allows the producer to view a whole video clip (in low resolution) while looking at the accompanying script on another part of the screen. CNN has a similar service, but it is too expensive for KTNV. ABC's regional feeds can be brought up as separate files, which is important because KTNV producers are primarily interested in stories developed by stations in the Pacific and Mountain time zones. Video editors read text rundowns and pull stories off the feeds according to their position in the feed.

The 6:30 p.m. producer has been trying to reach a freelance entertainment reporter who works 2 days a week and who is supposed to have a feature for this evening. He hopes to have a rundown put together by 3 p.m., at which point he can turn in his order for graphics, and begin to write the on-camera and voice-over copy, as well as the teasers, that go at the end of each section of the broadcast.

One helpful feature of the computer system software is a *lock function* that registers each script to a specific broadcast. Only one person can work on the script at a time, and the *status bar* on the producer's rundown tells who last read the script. One dot means a reporter read (or worked on it) the script, two dots indicate an anchor read it, three dots mean the producer read it. There is also a color code: Three green dots mean it's approved and ready for air, a red dot means it is not approved, and a yellow code means someone has changed the script since the producer checked it.

There are eight reporters and nine photographers on duty. People are beginning to filter into the newsroom. There are two nightside reporters. They are supervised by a managing editor and producers. The assignment desk normally has two editors, but both recently left for new jobs, and the managing editor and the operations manager are filling in on the assignment desk.

The newsgathering hardware includes three ENG trucks and a helicopter.

The 6:30 p.m. producer is checking to make sure the 6:30 p.m. is not repeating too much from the 6 p.m. lineup. At 2:20 p.m. the entertainment reporters calls in, responding to a beeper message. She will have her feature ready in time for the 6:30 p.m. broadcast.

The NewStar computer system has an archives feature. The 5 p.m. producer complains that someone did not put a number on a file, making it difficult to find an item in the archives.

At 2:54 p.m., the promotions writer drops by to discuss topical promotion spots for the 6:30 p.m. broadcast.

3:01 p.m.: There is concern in the newsroom about doing three remotes from the helicopter from different locations between 5 and 7 p.m. One producer points out the helicopter may not carry enough fuel to fly as far as needed without taking time out to refuel.

3:07 p.m.: The 6:30 p.m. producer turns in his graphics request.

The assignment desk says Reno is feeding the prisoner shot story to CNN at 4:30 p.m.

The 6:30 p.m. producer is on the telephone, trying to find out whether fuel capacity would limit the helicopter's ability to cover three locations this afternoon. The 6:30 p.m. helicopter story would be about a new stretch of interstate highway that is being closed to traffic all next week so stunts can be shot for a movie.

By 3:11 p.m., the tempo of activity in the newsroom has picked up noticeably.

3:17 p.m.: The rundown shows the program is overtime by 30 seconds.

The producers are still debating how to do three live shots at 5, 6, and 6:30 p.m. The 6:30 p.m. producer decides to drop the helicopter live shot because it is a cloudy day and it may be too dark for a live shot by 6:30 p.m.

The news director walks through the newsroom, but doesn't intervene in any of the activity.

The broadcast is now under by 10 seconds. The producer writes a couple of extra stories that can be dropped. The helicopter has been shooting at the Clark County Fair, which is some distance from Las Vegas.

The wire (seen on the producer's computer screen) carries a snow advisory for the mountains of Southern Nevada. The producer talks with the weather forecaster by telephone. The forecaster downplays the risk during the telephone conversation and takes an equally cautious view during his first evening weather segment.

The producer is typing headlines for the anchors. These have to be prerecorded because the anchor teams change at 6:30 p.m. and recorded headlines are played on the station break to allow the new anchors time to slip into their seats. The co-anchors tape the headlines at 4 p.m.

Normally each broadcast has a different director, but today one director is out, so the 6 p.m. director will also direct the 6:30 p.m. broadcast. He won't have very much time to look over the script and rundown for the 6:30 broadcast.

It's almost time for the 5 p.m. news to go on the air, and everyone is in motion, so we quietly leave.

CONCLUSION

Television news is highly technical and extensively automated. Although the total available audience for television news in the United States is fairly constant, new news services continue to be introduced. This growth of services requires greater efficiency and less human intervention in production. It also places a tremendous emphasis on producers, who are a scarce commodity in the employment market due to the special talents needed and the stressful complexity of the job. Producing continues to increase in importance as a source of senior managers. A student journalist would be wise to look at producing as an exciting, rewarding part of broadcast journalism that offers ample opportunities for career advancement.

5
The Production Team

Producing Television news is a team effort. In the next few chapters, you will learn about the synthesis involving the producer, specific members of the production team and the technology they use.

THE REPORTER/WRITER/ANCHOR WORK STATION

Reporters, writers, and anchors have different organizational duties, but they use their computer terminals for similar tasks. They rely on the newsroom computer system to help them find source copy, do research, exchange messages, receive mail, write stories, view and edit video, and send completed work to the producer.

SEARCHING THE WIRES

One of the basic tasks broadcast journalists perform at computer terminals is checking the press agency wires for relevant copy. Practically everyone in the newsroom does this at one time or another during the day.

In the early 1970s the two main U.S. news services, The Associated Press (AP) and United Press International (UPI) began to convert their internal traffic systems and distribution networks to data feeds. Eventually chattering teletype machines were removed from subscriber newsrooms, and high-speed dot-matrix printers were installed. This not only permitted the press agencies to make their internal operations more efficient, it allowed them to deliver copy at a higher speed. In turn, subscribers benefited from receiving news copy faster and in greater quantity.

From there the wire services moved to offering specialized menus of copy, sorted and prepared according to the perceived needs of users. This meant that instead of a major newsroom having to install a printer for each wire: national-international ("A" wire), supplemental ("B" wire), state, business, and sports, all of these categories could be programmed to be sent to one computer printer.

High-speed delivery of selected material to fast, reasonably quiet computer printers was better than having several noisy teletype machines clacking away in the background at a tortuous rate of 66-words-per-minute. The problem with the new DataStream service was that it spewed yards and yards of printer paper every hour. Anyone who needed to read the wire had too much paper to scan to find the specific items of interest.

The development of newsroom computer systems for broadcasters presented the press agencies with solutions to two problems, a paper glut in newsrooms and high costs for maintenance services. Once newsroom computers became common, the wire service feed was delivered to the computer instead of a wire service printer. The newsroom computer stored all the wire stories and automatically deleted old files at set intervals. Wire service items were coded so that the newsroom computer could sort incoming copy into categories. A story could be quickly found by scanning lists of story categories and titles. The computer systems also contained briefs that described the current stories on file. Once a story was selected, it could be retrieved to the terminal screen, and if desired, a hard copy could be printed out.

The wire services' second problem was the huge cost of providing printers and printer service to customers. Once newsroom computer systems became common, the press agencies' technical responsibility ended when the data signal arrived at the TV station, either by satellite or wire.

No matter how the software is written, each newsroom system vendor has a method to recognize the sorting codes and classify incoming wire stories so that they can be filed by the computer. This is why a journalist coming into a new newsroom must learn how to access wire copy on that newsroom's system. It's a fundamental task for reporters, writers, editors, producers, and anchors.

Typically, a writer or reporter goes to the wire service briefs or summaries soon after they sit down at the terminal. These provide an overview of what's going on in their area of interest, which might be a city, the state, the nation, or even the world. If you're working in sports, then it's the sports summary, in business, the business summary.

If a story shows up which is of interest, the reporter or writer opens the item on the screen. Some people work from copy on the screen, others print out a copy. That's frequently a question of what works best for the user. A reporter might want to take a paper copy of a story along while covering a story.

Producers, production assistants, assignment editors, and writers use the wires to search for a specific topic, or a specific news story. This is useful when you need to build a background file on a story or because you want to: (a) write a roundup, that is, do a story which gives information about similar occurrences, such as a string of arson fires involving churches; or (b) you find a regional or national story and decide to develop a local angle, such as an item about the government ordering military bases closed.

Press agency copy is used in many ways. At the network level, there is a preference for writing from what is called *source copy*. Traditionally the wire services have produced long newspaper-style items first when a new story breaks. In addition, the major stories are rewritten and updated for each daily 12-hour cycle, based on the needs of morning and afternoon newspapers. The Associated Press rewrites from its own long-form stories to produce broadcast-style (ready for reading) copy for broadcast subscribers. (United Press International no longer functions as a worldwide general-purpose press agency.)

Network news writers used newspaper-style stories for reference when they are writing. Famed CBS News Correspondent Walter Cronkite was fond of telling journalists the lead or beginning to a story, for a television broadcast might be hidden in the seventeenth paragraph of a piece of wire copy.

Networks use other sources, such as a second or third press agency's copy, transcripts of stories prepared by their own staff or by affiliates, and information developed by their own desk staff. Theoretically, a well-resourced network newsroom in the United States would have access to several of the AP services, Reuters (an international service based in Britain), and financial wires. Some large news organizations subscribe to Agence France Presse (AFP), an international news service based in France. Almost all news organizations make use of Internet sources.

One of the outstanding examples of a network that has vast information resources is the British Broadcasting Corporation, the quasigovernment noncommercial portion of Britain's broadcast community. The BBC's latest newsroom computer system is designed to give its journalists almost instant access to a wealth of resources, which might include:

Press Agencies: The Associated Press (AP)

Reuters

Agence France Presse (AFP, France)

AFP Domestic in French

Press Association (PA, UK domestic)

Press Association Sports

Reuters Financial

TASS (Russia)

Press Trust of India (PTI)

Extel Financial

Extel Sports

Central Office of Information (COI)—a feed from British government ministries.

Internal: AMS—distributes local agency material to the BBC regional centers.

BBC Material—feed of material prepared by BBC journalists. It includes general copy in addition to material from an internal news service feeding the regions, political, economic, traffic and BBC sport units.

Caversham. Two feeds from the BBC Monitoring Service, which monitors broadcasts worldwide and packages information for the BBC.

(BBC World Service [shortwave] also takes several foreign language services)[1]

Archives: A fabulous storehouse of information, audio and video.

If anything, a BBC journalist might be faced with having too much information available.

Another resource that most newsrooms include on desk terminals is the Internet. A journalist who understands how to use the Internet to access information has amazing resources. More information about computer-assisted reporting can be found in chapter 9 (this volume).

A local television station or cable newsroom in the United States would subscribe to fewer services. The Associated Press is the major supplier of news agency services in the United States. Some of its offerings include:

AP TV Wire—A 7-day-a-week, 24-hour-a-day service for TV stations. The service provides detailed print-style stories, plus ready-to-air broadcast scripts and separate items. The APTV News Wire is selectable by news category so it can be customized to suit a newsroom's needs. The choices include:

In-depth state news wire.

In-depth national and international news wires.

The AP NewsPower news wire.

The AP Sports wire.

The Planner—a list of major national and international news events, current and future. It includes contact names and telephone numbers.

Washington Daybook—planned events.

State Daybook—planned events and coverage in the subscriber's state.

Bulletins.

Adjacent state coverage.

Weather—forecasts, temperatures, weather bulletins.

Sports including statistics.

Business stories, market averages, agriculture news.

Entertainment news.

Lottery results.

Features.

Optional Services

Full AP DataStream—all the latest news

---

[1]Information supplied by BBC News & Current Affairs, August, 1998.

THE PRODUCTION TEAM

Additional state newspaper-style reports

Canadian news

Spanish-language news

AP Alert Wire—a computer scans approximately 10,000 AP stories from all states and around the nation and world to fit 10 special categories

AP Sports wire (full-time)

AP Business (full-time)

AP Express—a shared data network installed free at stations, the cost is paid by organizations and companies wishing to distribute news releases.

AP TV NewsPower—a basic, fully scripted news wire written in broadcast style. It includes national and international news, weather, sports, entertainment and business from the home state, plus two adjacent states. It includes planning guides, bulletins, weather, sports, business and entertainment news.

Television Headlines—The service delivers the day's most important news stories in broadcast style. This is a cut-down economy service.

APTV—A video syndication service operated by the AP. You may see references to this service on the AP wires.

FIG. 5.1. Many of the services provided by The Associated Press to broadcasters originate in the AP Broadcast Center in Washington, DC. Image courtesy of The Associated Press.

That is a long list, but it serves to illustrate the enormous quantity and variety of information that can be routed through a newsroom terminal, dependent on the needs and budget of a news organization.

Now you have an idea of the power of the tools you will be using. The more you learn about searching the wires from any terminal to which you are assigned, the better off you will be.

A COMPUTER FILE CABINET

The newsroom computer can be a major labor-saver in terms of keeping files. Writers and reporters, especially reporters, tend to keep informal files on topics with which they deal frequently. Before computers, the filing system frequently consisted of newspaper clippings and carbon copies of script pages shoved into a file folder that ended up in an over-stuffed file drawer.

Newsroom computer systems approach the issue of keeping files differently, but all will have a method for you to keep files of information that you might need later. One way to help yourself is to remember to save all scripts you write and assign the ones that may be useful in the future to specific computer files. Saving scripts is important, not only for your future reference, but in case the system "eats" your script at some other stage. You would at least be able to resurrect the copy you submitted to your producer.

Reporters who cover specific *beats*—which are areas of interest such as education, or places, such as city hall—find it useful to be able to quickly look back and see

FIG. 5.2. Reporters in the field like this video journalist from New York 1 can use portable computers or personal data assistants (PDA) to retrieve information in the newsroom computer system. Photo courtesy of Panasonic Broadcast & Television Systems Company.

THE PRODUCTION TEAM   75

what took place 2 weeks or 2 months ago. It's usually easier to find a fact in your own script. Some reporters scan documents they acquire into their files for easy retrieval.

One thing all writers and reporters should do is keep extensive files of contact names and contact information. The newsroom computer, as well as smaller portable devices, are a big help in organizing personal information.

DATA SERVICES

Two names that pop up frequently when data services are discussed are Lexis™ and Nexis™. Lexis is a database of law information. One can quickly and efficiently search for relevant cases, a task which can be frustrating and time-consuming when done by looking through law books on library shelves. Nexis is a news database. Many database searches are done by giving the computer a key word and then gradually narrowing the search. Both services have subscription fees and are most likely to show up in a major market or network newsrooms. The trend is to do searches on the Internet. A reporter or writer should not do a search involving fees until permission has been obtained from the management.

Another type of database is the CD, or compact disk. It is possible to buy an encyclopedia in compact disk form. There are CDs available that have many useful databases, such as detailed maps, addresses, or telephone directories. This information can also be located on the Internet.

One of the most useful aspects of the Internet is its connection to the files of public agencies. Many federal, state, and local agencies are distributing information or opening files to computer-equipped members of the public. It is a major project for a public agency to convert its records to the form needed for computer retrieval, but after the work is done, a great deal of manual searching is eliminated and the public is better served. It is important that someone in the newsroom organize information about public information sites. Most states include information kept in computer files under their *open records laws,* meaning the public must have access to these files.

MESSAGES

Message-exchange is a feature of a networked newsroom computer system that is heavily used. Most vendors supply an internal message system that helps to bridge the communication gaps that occur in TV newsrooms when people work across a 7-day, around-the-clock schedule.

A message system may be a special internal service or it may rely on off-the-shelf e-mail technology. It is not difficult for a savvy computer user to access your messages, so never write something that you might regret later or that might lead to trouble between you and another employee or a manager.

What are the common sorts of messages?

- Calls received in the newsroom: It never seems to fail, someone calls for you and you aren't where you can be located at that moment. You are

more likely to get an accurate message when the person answering the phone can type the message on their terminal, and then send it to your "mailbox."
- Memos to the staff from managers: It's one way of making certain that everyone *should* be aware of a new policy.
- Alerts: Wire service alerts (urgent, bulletin, flash), network alerts, and newsroom urgent messages can be directed to all terminals. Many systems place these messages at the top of the terminal screen, no matter what function is running on the terminal at the time.
- Pass-along information: Many times a producer on the early morning shift wants to leave information for the daytime or evening producer. The message system makes doing it quick and easy.
- Messages can be left for newsroom staff from remote locations, bureaus, mobile units, and home.
- Messages that come from external sources can be copied and transferred to the internal network for sharing with other staff members.
- Message systems lower the frustration level in large newsrooms. Answering the phone ties up production workers, and frustrates producers. It's better for a producer to write a message saying "Please recut Florida forest fire to :30 for VO in 3 p.m. segment." The tape editor can message back, "Florida fire VO :30, 3 p.m. ready."
- Widespread advisories: During an observation visit to the CNN newsroom in Atlanta there was a great deal of discussion among producers about gaining access to their White House Correspondent for a live question and answer session with an anchorperson. At one point the live shot was set up for the 4 to 4:30 p.m. news, when a message flashed at the top of screens throughout the newsroom: "WH correspondent unavailable for 4, moved to 5 to 6 p.m. special." The 4 p.m. producer wasn't happy, but the quick notice gave his team time to make a substitution without creating a panic situation.
- Training reminders: Especially in large organizations, it is critical to make sure everyone has attended mandatory training sessions.
- Feed alerts: Many TV newsrooms have such a heavy inflow of satellite feed offerings that it is difficult to inform key personnel when something special is going to happen. A message such as: "President holds previously unannounced live press briefing at 11 a.m. EST today" is guaranteed to get a reaction.

WRITING

The computer terminal is, before anything else, a place where writing is done. Newsroom computer system vendors install a variety of word-processing programs, but most have been built around Windows® software from Microsoft® Corporation. Based on experiences shared by a wide variety of users, I have compiled a list of problem areas that you might encounter when writing on a terminal:

One important rule: Do not depend on software to fix all of your typos and grammar errors. Remember, you are the smart one, the computer is essentially dumb. If you type *s i t e* when you mean *c i t e,* the computer will not make a correction because it has not been programmed to figure out context. By the way, the program being used to write this paragraph made both letter *i*'s into capital *I* because it had been set to assume an isolated letter (*i*) was a personal pronoun. Most journalism copy is double spaced. This may require setting the word-processing program to double space.

Save copy frequently unless your word-processor has an absolutely safe automatic save function. Many new computer users lose valuable documents because they forget to assign a "file" or place to store the document. One trick that sometimes gets you out of trouble when looking for a lost document in a DOS-based word-processing program is to look for your document with a .BAK ending. So if you can't find citycom.doc (city commission. document) but you are certain you opened a file, then ask the program to find citycom.bak (city commission backup). Word-processing programs with automatic back-up will save it, but you may need some help accessing the backup file. In Windows programs, if you click on File ... Save As ... you will see a spot under the name of the file you are saving called *Save as type.* If you scroll this window you will see some of the other possible files.

If your computer uses a Windows program, you can learn a lot of interesting tricks for storing, restoring, and moving copy. Those windows can be friendly or they can drive you crazy. One common problem is covering up one or more windows with other windows. This can be helped by doing two things: First, after you are through reading a document, close it so it isn't hanging around in the background. Second, many of these programs allow you to *maximize* or *minimize* a window. The maximize function fills your whole screen with one work area. Minimize uses only a portion of the total screen, and if you learn how to move the small screens around, you can have several little screens in front of you at one time. (Of course, you may not be able to read them!)

The other function that needs to be mastered is the *print* function. Your program may require you to pick which printer you want to use. It may also ask you for the number of copies you want run off. Many of these programs allow you to print a whole document, or any number of pages from the document. In Windows programs, learn how to access the **Print Manager** function. It will help you fix a printing problem. Type faces are usually standard in newsroom computer software, but if your program has an active option, find out the type face is required in your newsroom. Many newsrooms use several different printers. They may use a high-capacity page printer for copies of short documents and rundowns, while running multipage, multicopy scripts on a high-speed dot-matrix printer.

Under **Edit** in the list of categories at the top of some Windows screen, two commands are hidden that can be very useful. They are **Copy** and **Paste**. In most cases you *highlight* (use your mouse to blacken) copy you would like to move and click on **Copy**. You then move the pointer to the new location and click on **Paste**. This is very handy for pulling excerpts out of archives or wire copy or for moving a sentence or paragraph that seems out of place. You must be sure that the copy you drop in fits grammatically, and you must delete it from its original location. Otherwise, you may end up repeating yourself. The **Copy** and **Paste** commands are useful when you want to send text within an e-mail message, or pull text out of e-mail. Another function, found under **File** is **Send To**, which leads you to **Mail Recipient** or **Mail Recipient (as Attachment)**. This allows you to e-mail selected text or documents.

The command **Go To** under **Edit** gives you a quick way to return to the beginning of a document (or reach any other part of the document). Just answer the questions **Go To** asks you, and you will be all set.

You will find the spelling and grammar checkers under **Tools**. Be certain the spelling checker is set for the language you are using (e.g., English US). There is a lot more to be learned about the typical Windows operating system, but the highlights mentioned here are some of the more frequently used functions.

BUILDING PACKAGES AT THE PC

It is necessary to generalize about producing a television package at a newsroom computer system terminal because there are variations from one vendor's product to another, and from newsroom to newsroom.

The first task is to write the script. The work begins just a soon as you get the assignment. For a reporter, it means researching the story and beginning to conceptualize how is might be told for television. A writer needs to do a thorough *read-in,* that is, make certain he or she understands exactly what the story is about and what materials are available with which to tell the story.

The more you know, the better you do. The visual side of a television story is absolutely critical, so you should go through a mental checklist:

1. How much time has been allocated in the broadcast for this story?
2. What instructions do we have from the producer?
3. What do we have for video? How long is each scene? What is said in the interviews?
4. How might this story be introduced? Should we use a still Chromakey or dissolve from a freeze-frame to the tape?
5. Who was interviewed? What are their names and titles? Any locations to be identified?
6. Where was this shot? What did the background look and sound like?
7. Is there anything missing that we can find out by virtue of talking to one of our staff members, making a phone call, or looking for an information source?
8. How about background information—what happened before, or what led up to this story?

9. Do we need file video from the archives?
10. Is there any forward angle—a public hearing, a court appearance?
11. Does this story tie to anything else current in the news?

Many newsroom computer systems are also automation systems. Assume you will have to insert the video instructions and likely you will have to *imbed* (i.e., type or press specially designated keys on the keyboard) video (and audio) machine-control cues in the script. Today, the writer/reporter is frequently responsible for accurately listing all the visuals and providing the information needed for automated production. One simple, but very important, task is to make certain all CGs are correct, with the person's name and title, or the location name spelled correctly. Even if your newsroom is not automated, the director is going to need to know exactly what visuals go with the piece and where they should be inserted.

There is a growing trend toward installing terminals that can display low-resolution moving video of locally shot stories or video from feeds. You could be required to produce a "shot list" based on the video you have viewed. The final editing from the shot list may be done by a trained editor, who will work from your instructions, but there is a trend toward having writers and reporters pull up the video and actually do editing on their workstations.

CNN in Atlanta installed a fiber optic cable network throughout its newsroom. This technology enables reporters and writers to share and browse (look at) video in low-resolution ("low-res"). The video comes from CNN's 36 international bureaus and 700 affiliates (Kienzle, 1998).[2] When the video seen on a workstation looks the same as it does on a playback monitor, it is called high-resolution or "high-res."

We are talking about focusing a great deal more work and expecting a wide variety of talents, at the writer's or reporter's desk—not just writing, but integrating the script, cutting the tape, and producing the finished story. At a minimum, this calls on reporting, writing, graphics, video editing, and producing skills, all bundled into one writer/reporter. This is a daunting assortment of skills for someone to possess.

A news executive from HTV West, a commercial television station in Bristol, England and Cardiff (Wales) described management's reasoning for installing advanced browsing technology, during a conference in Germany in 1998. He said: "The one thing we wanted above all was desktop editing. Journalists are used to telling video editors what they want in a story, so we said, why not bring the creative power right into the hands of journalists—they're already using a newsroom computer anyway, manipulating text, so why not manipulate video, graphics and everything else?" (Radlo, 1997, p. 19)

Once you are finished with your piece, it should be put in a file for review by the producer, who may ask for some changes. Once approved by the producer, the finished piece is *in the can* (an old film term for it being done and ready to transmit). You will probably instruct your terminal to send it to a digital server where the produced piece will rest in a computer's memory until the director calls for it. (Alterna-

---

[2]The text author observed the system in use in January, 1998.

tively, the story might be recorded on tape and transferred to an automated videotape playback unit.)

FIELD REPORTING

Laptop computers have made it possible to move the newsroom computer system terminal into the field. Reporters can connect their laptop using a telephone line, or a satellite circuit, to the main system through a dial-up modem or via the Internet. Some news departments now equip reporters with smaller, hand-held devices that can be linked to the newsroom computer system. This connectivity means a reporter can read wire copy and instructions, and share a draft of a script with a producer or editor in the newsroom. Many of the microwave vans and mobile satellite trucks we see today have connections to tie a portable computer to the public telephone system (or a satellite channel) and then into the main newsroom computer system.

The development of small portable digital video editors makes it possible to shoot, edit, script and produce a video news story in the field, either in a remote site, a microwave van or a satellite truck. This means that the reporter and technician(s) do not need to come into the newsroom during the day. Some television stations have eliminated offices for bureaus, and relying on the ENG/SNV vehicles functioning as bureaus.

FIG. 5.3. Portable digital video editors can be taken to the scene of a news story. Some combine editing capability with other functions of a newsroom system terminal so that stories can be written, edited, and transmitted from the same terminal. This technology was used extensively in the second Iraq War. Photo courtesy of Panasonic Broadcast & Television Systems Company.

THE PRODUCTION TEAM

One concern that grows out of this technology is the increasing difficulty editors and producers have in getting material from these rolling bureaus into the newsroom in time to make or request revisions.

ANCHOR TERMINALS

The majority of anchorpersons working in television news have journalistic backgrounds and training. The computer terminal is an everyday tool in their work. Anchors need a computer terminal on their desk in order to read the wires, write or preview copy, and check the program rundown.

Involvement in the Process

The next time you watch a major news broadcast try counting the number of terminals you can see, and note whether or not there is one on the anchor desk. Some anchors' computer screens are built into the desk, others use a laptop.

The primary uses of the anchor terminal combine functions found on both the journalist's terminal and the producer's terminal.

Anchors observed at CNN spent a great deal of time in front of the camera, so their main need for computer terminals was to scan the news wires, view rundowns, and preview copy. When CNN anchors are not in the live studio, they are likely to be recording segments or recording material for other services, such as the CNN Airport Channel.

Weather anchors at the Weather Channel in Atlanta, Georgia prepare their own rundowns and select the data and data screens they need for their segments. The weather anchors are meteorologists who create their segments in a database, and then insert the information into the running order. They use a newsroom computer

FIG. 5.4. Anchors at the Weather Channel in Atlanta rely on the latest computer technology to help compile and present their forecasts. Photo courtesy of The Weather Channel.

system, plus special software needed for weather presentations. The on-camera meteorologists use a hand-held control to run the segment from the studio.

In larger markets the news anchors frequently have heavy on-air responsibilities, requiring them to focus more on performance than reporting or writing. Many stations encourage their anchors to participate in public service activities, which can be time consuming. At WTVT-TV in Tampa, anchors sometimes write, but writing is not a primary activity for the Fox station's anchors.

An anchorperson wrote to the e-mail newsletter *ShopTalk*, describing some of an anchor's responsibilities.

The writer said: "In our shop, I write a few stories each night, tweak, then cut what seems to be a never-ending stream of promos and updates, then go into the scripts an hour before the broadcast.

"Once there, I edit/rearrange/blow-up/rewrite/correct, do whatever it takes to make the story understandable and 'lawsuit free.'" (Our producers and reporters do a fine job, but mistakes are made. Conversely, I hope they catch the errors I make.)

"Then it's my job to communicate ... make that 'connect' ... with the audience, and I'd better do a better job than the people across town, or I'm the one who gets canned!"

In smaller markets people double up on jobs within the news department. Sometimes the anchors act as producers, writing copy and developing the lineup. Anchors working on nonprime time broadcasts, such as the morning news frequently have to write part of the script. Other smaller size markets encourage their anchorpeople to report, either doing one story a day, or by developing features and special series. There are markets where the news director is also the lead anchor.

Producers, anchors, and reporters participated in the twice-daily planning meetings at WTXL-TV, in Tallahassee, Florida. This is typical of the less structured environment found in smaller news departments.

Many people in broadcast news serve as anchor/reporters, splitting their time between reporting days and anchoring days, usually carrying out their anchor functions on weekends. Weekday anchors frequently work on special reports or features.

The pattern in recent years has been for reporters to gain experience and then take on the challenge of anchoring weekend or morning broadcasts to develop the skills they will need when the opportunity to move into a full time prime anchor slot comes their way.

In contrast to the way network anchors are presented in movies, the majority are experienced journalists and at least one has the additional title of "managing editor," which gives the anchorperson authority over the content and style of the broadcast.

Today's news anchors are involved in the process of gathering and organizing the news for their broadcasts. They have the same capabilities to do research, review wire copy, write stories, review video, and read rundowns as writers and producers have built into their terminals.

Using the Terminal in the Studio

The newsroom computer system provides two streams of information to the anchors in the studio, instructions, and the script. The script in the newsroom com-

FIG. 5.5. This anchorperson is using an older prompter that projects the script onto a mirror from which the anchor reads. The camera's taking lens gets an unimpeded shot through the back of the mirror, which is like surveillance mirrors used in retail stores. Newer prompters use flat-screen computer monitors mounted above the camera lens.

puter system is routed to special software that drives the prompter. Prompting devices usually feed a large-type version of the script to a TV monitor suspended below the lens of a camera. The image is reflected on a one-way mirror mounted in front of the camera lens. The talent can read both instructions and the script on the mirror surface, while the lens picks up the picture through the back of the one-way mirror. (These are the same types of mirrors that are used in retail stores for surveillance.) The point to this technique is that an anchorperson can maintain eye contact. Each viewer is led to think the anchorperson is speaking directly to him or her.

Most anchors have a terminal installed in their on-air desk. This can be used as a secondary prompter, or it can be set for messaging or to show the rundown. This arrangement facilitates the process of making changes in the rundown or script, providing the presenter is comfortable reading a rundown. Typically, when a change is made in most rundowns, the newsroom system automatically reorders all the information on the screen and retimes the broadcast. This saves a lot of conversation on the intercommunication system (usually referred to as the IFB, or interruptible fold back). Another advantage to having a terminal at the anchor desk is that changes that occur in the minutes just before the broadcast goes live are relatively easy to share with everyone concerned. The anchors and producer are less cut off from the newsroom.

If a major story breaks during the newscast, it can be sent to the anchor on the computer screen. Usually the first indication of a breaking story is relayed on the anchor's earpiece, which is connected to the control room intercommunication circuit.

CARE AND FEEDING OF ANCHORS

Although computer technology makes it easier to anchor and produce a complex news broadcast, there are human-relations aspects to the producer–anchor team that are essential to the success of the program. We shall look at the team primarily from the viewpoint of the producer.

An anchor has to establish a "relationship" with the audience. Some of that relationship creates empathy between the presenter and the viewer. People trust their favorite anchorperson. They may feel the anchorperson is part of their community, even part of their family. It is this sort of loyalty that builds an audience, and therefore ratings, for stations and networks. The higher the ratings, the higher the advertising rates. Successful anchorpersons make money for their organizations, and this is why good anchors are paid well for their unique combination of technical and presentation skills.

Anchoring the news is about performance. Performance involves a number of skills, which must be combined in such a way that an anchorperson is technically skilled, yet human. Viewers must trust and respect an anchorperson. Appearance is important, and the technical limitations of television require close attention to color and texture. Anchors have to wear makeup in most studio settings to offset the intensity of the lights. Hair should stay in place, no matter how much the anchorperson moves around. Clothing and accessories are very important but should not be so distracting that they divert the viewer's attention from the news. A

THE PRODUCTION TEAM

sparkling diamond pendant can wipe out a camera shot due to the intensity of the light reflected off the stone. A stick-pin in a tie can rub against a microphone. There is a lot of detail to be considered by an anchorperson.

What are some of the skills an anchorperson must develop?

1. Reading from written copy in a well-modulated voice, giving careful attention to diction, expression, and pacing.
2. Excellent knowledge of verbal grammar and correct pronunciation.
3. Stage presence—the ability to appear natural and relaxed whether or not you are. Knowing how to move, use facial expressions, and use body language.
4. Self-assurance sufficient to cope with change and crises while appearing calm.
5. The ability to talk extemporaneously—especially about news-related topics. A solid knowledge of current events.

Producers frequently complain about anchorpersons' egos. Ego and self-assurance are necessary to function as a performer, and anchoring is performing. The same qualities can be seen in successful salespersons, high-powered executives, and outstanding foreign correspondents. Each must first master their trade before being a "spokesperson."

Some anchors count the number of seconds they are on the air compared to their coanchor. Producers learn to live with this type of behavior. If it becomes destructive to the news product, it is up to the news director to intervene.

Anchors complain about producers who believe the broadcast is "their" property. A producer pours heart and soul into the broadcast, and a producer has the right to be proud of a good product. But, television news is based on teamwork. Producers, directors, anchors, technicians, editors, writers, videographers, and production assistants all have to pull together in order to have a successful broadcast.

Two words producers should remember: *advice* and *praise*. Encourage team members to offer advice and make suggestions. Where practical, take the suggestion and run. When a suggestion isn't going to work, thank the person, and explain why you won't be able to act on it. Praise people for all the good things they do, and do it frequently.

In the early years of a producer's career, she or he may be working with anchors who have many more years of experience that the producer. They can be an outstanding source of background on local stories, and how things have been done in the past. Some anchors are perfectionists, and they will correct grammatical errors that the producer has missed. Think of it this way, you may have had to gracefully accept criticism, but that's one less error, one less phone call, or one less e-mail message from a local member of the "grammar police."

Before you criticize, make certain you are right. That's what dictionaries and pronunciation guides are for. It is humiliating for a producer when the anchor produces a copy of the *NBC Handbook of Pronunciation* and turns out to be right.

Anchors are particularly sensitive to what works and what doesn't work. They usually know the technical and personnel limitations of the facility, and therefore, can guide a producer through a minefield of potential problems.

Encourage your anchors to be actively involved in the process of preparing the news. They should be using their terminal to read the wires for background. Anchors should read two or more major newspapers a day. They should sit in on production and planning meetings when possible. They should look over copy, especially difficult copy, well before broadcast time. Encourage your anchors to think up questions to toss to field reporters during live remotes. Most anchors want to preserve their credentials as journalists. Treat people as you would want them to treat you.

Warn your anchors if you anticipate doing a live interview from the studio or a remote location. An interviewer needs to "read in" to a story or issue in order to be effective during a live interview. Most live interviews you see on network TV, especially on the morning programs, have been set up well ahead of time. If possible, a writer or associate producer has already done a preinterview with the guest, and a researcher has prepared a background on the interviewee and the subject for use by the anchorperson. When a live interview falters, it may be because someone did not provide the anchorperson with sufficient or accurate information. How does this happen? Frequently a live-interview mismatch occurs when a field producer is desperately looking for someone to be interviewed, and after finding someone, oversells the idea to a harassed producer at network headquarters who fails to get adequately briefed. The studio producer needs to be certain she or he understands who is being interviewed and what information the person has to share with viewers.

It takes courage, but there are times when an interview opportunity needs to be passed by, or delayed until all the parties understand what information is available. Nothing looks or sounds worse than an anchorperson misidentifying the interviewee or asking an irrelevant question. Don't sandbag the talent, give the anchors time to prepare.

FIG. 5.6. Anchors on a set at the cable network, CNBC. Note the fluorescent lighting panels at the top of the set. Lighting is one of the director's responsibilities.

One network morning anchor kept referring to the officer in charge of a state's National Guard units in direct address as "Major General —." He was correctly identified at the beginning of the live shot as a Major General, but when asking questions, the anchor should have said: "General —." A small gaffe, but one that is irritating to thousands of viewers who have served in the military.

It is not unusual for a producer to provide possible questions that an anchor can use during a live interview. Two major errors can be observed: (1) the line of questioning displays a lack of knowledge on the part of the person who wrote them; (2) The questions break some of the simple rules of interviewing, including the following:

- Do not ask compound questions, that is, questions with two parts. The interviewee has the option of answering (1) the easier part, or (2) the last part of the question because that is all he or she remembers.
- Do not phrase a question so that it begs an answer. (When did you stop hitting your husband?)
- Make the wording of your question simple and direct. Not only do you want to elicit a strong response, you are having to overcome the interviewee's difficulties in hearing the interviewer over the IFB (private communication channel between the studio and the person being interviewed).
- Ask only what you think the interviewee can answer. If the interviewee was a passenger on a burning cruise ship, you wouldn't ask what *kind or type* of fire it was unless the person were qualified to label the blaze.
- Do not ask the interviewee to evaluate the legality or correctness of someone's conduct, unless they are qualified. Even then, be cautious so that your employer doesn't end up on the wrong side of a libel suit.
- Do not bias your question based on your or someone else's personal opinion. Your question should not assume criminal conduct or evil motives.
- If there is one irritating trait common to inexperienced producers, writers, reporters, and anchors, it is asking questions that demonstrate ignorance, lack of information, or an assumption not warranted by known facts. All politicians are not crooks, police don't necessarily practice brutality, and businesspersons are not universally greedy. Perhaps it could be generalized by saying that these questions frequently lack the quality we call "common sense."

CONCLUSION

The computer terminal on your desk is a lot more than an electronic typewriter. Depending on how expert you become in utilizing its software, it can become a production center. This requires that you not only learn how to employ the functions of software; you must learn what constitutes a good "edit"; what is an effective CG; how to mix and match voice-over tape, tape with wild sound, and sound-on-tape to tell a story. In other words, what you are doing involves artistic and intellectual skills beyond simply stringing sentences together.

Anyone going to work in television news today has to be well acquainted with personal computers and computer-assisted reporting and research. A smart producer looks out for and protects his or her anchorpeople. If the anchor makes a mistake, save your criticism for a private moment. Above all, avoid literal egg-on-the-face situations. If your female anchor has forgotten one earring, tell her. Remind the male anchor to straighten his tie. Looks mean a lot when you face a great unseen audience every night. Viewers do notice little details.

A healthy ego generally helps an anchorperson to do his or her job. The anchor must also remember that the rest of the team is not working solely for his or her benefit and visibility, but to bring the best news product to the audience. The anchor is a vehicle for this product.

6

The Assignment Desk

The assignment desk in a busy television newsroom is an exciting place, the heartbeat of the operation. The assignment desk organizes stories, dispatches crews, deploys equipment, and is always ready to discard the plan for the day when important news breaks. A television news operation that doesn't have a well-organized assignment desk is in trouble.

A great deal of the daily work on an assignment desk is made up of unrelenting routine. The beat calls must be made. Important emergency service dispatchers must have their egos massaged. The wires must be read, so too the local newspapers, local periodicals, the e-mail, satellite and network feed briefings, and producers must be briefed on the results of routine inquiries.

When a true "breaking story" occurs, it is the assignment desk that makes or breaks the news operation. It must react swiftly and decisively. Follow-up must be skillful, thorough, and timely. Anyone who aims at a management job in broadcast news should spend some time on the assignment desk in order to understand the pulse of the news.

There is a genre of television news operations in which the emphasis is on spot news, and these operations need especially quick-witted assignment editors to call the shots.

KEEPING TRACK OF THINGS

The job of the assignment desk is to keep track of what is going on in the coverage area. This means:

1. Knowing what newsworthy events are currently taking place.
2. Following up on ongoing news stories.
3. Assembling information on future news stories/events.
4. Checking on public safety agencies to see if any of their activities are newsworthy.

5. Developing local tie-ins to news stories elsewhere.
6. Functioning as a "clearinghouse" for ideas that might yield stories.
7. Monitoring the political or governmental community.
8. Trolling "fringe areas" for stories.
9. Monitoring sources for breaking emergency situations.
10. Listening to stringers, neighborhood activists, outspoken citizens and anyone else who might call the desk.

The results of these efforts must be frequently and succinctly summarized for producers and news executives.

Newsworthy Events

The assignment desk is the clearinghouse for information on what is going on. The assignment desk issues lists of currently available stories and gives status reports on which ones are being covered and how. This is the basic information that provides the core for the producer's rundown.

The assignment desk may be staffed around the clock. The desk usually coordinates an early morning telephone conference call to brief key producers and managers on the day's rundown. At the beginning of the office day, a formal morning meeting is held, involving all of the top news management, including the Assignment Editor.

FIG. 6.1. The assignment desk at WTVT-TV in Tampa, Florida, takes up most of one wall in the newsroom. Photo by P. Keirstead.

THE ASSIGNMENT DESK

When we visited WTXL-TV, the ABC affiliate in Tallahassee, Florida, the Assignment Editor asked each reporter to give an update on his or her *beat* (i.e., the coverage for which the reporter is responsible) and then asked the reporter to comment on items in one of the several newspapers that arrive each morning. (Each reporter reads a specific paper.) Reporters were encouraged to contribute fresh ideas for stories, based on reading the newspaper or their own research. Some news directors demand that every reporter come to work each day with one or two story suggestions based on the reporter's reading and research. This system allows a small department to gather and filter a lot of information. A group discussion of this sort makes it possible for more experienced staff members to fill in newer staff.

At WTXL, the News Director and the Executive Producer participated actively in the morning meeting. The Assignment Editor also discussed the items already listed on the day's assignment sheet.

The assignment desk kept a rolling list of upcoming events that might warrant coverage. The newsroom computer is important for this function because it adapts well to storing this sort of data and changes in the list are easy to make. Some computer programs make provision for listing assignments on one screen, while printing out a specific instruction form for use by the reporter or videographer.

What kinds of events? Certain public bodies meet regularly. The assignment desk knows that the county commission meets Tuesdays, except the first Tuesday of the month. The desk adds the issues expected to be discussed to this routine entry, and in many instances, the Assignment Editor can extract the agenda for the meeting from the county web site, and transfer it to the assignment desk files.

Civic organizations plan events, some of which make interesting features. For example, a local service club that meets for lunch once a month may have the state's senior U.S. senator as next month's speaker. Certain dates are important, such as the graduation dates for the local high schools. Anniversaries make news, for instance, the 25th anniversary of the founding of a nearby community college. If a neighboring town is celebrating its 200th birthday, it might make an interesting story.

The desk also records calendar events such as the sentencing date in a sensational murder trial, the last day to file papers to run for local political office, the day the county storm water plan is supposed to be submitted to the Commission.

Where does the information come from?

Previous stories

The wire service calendar

Lists put out by civic bodies: cities, counties, school boards

The area's newspapers

News releases

Reporters and staff

Phone calls and tips

Web sites

Story/Date/Time	Resources	Details
A Schedule		Notes: Reporting: Rudy,Keith,Robyn,Erika,Ethan Contact: Phone: Location:
blimp crash folo		Notes: we need to find out who has arrived to investigate this crash...appears the cause is gusting winds..but you never know...what impact if any this will have the on the capitol classic..whether other balloon owners are worried about the weekend weather and if as a result this is going to be a bust of a weekend for the fest. bud leases the blimp from a company..the local(leasing) company rep. is katherine gomez who is here to be with the blimp for the fest is available 800-301-4726..she might be able to tell us what the dollar loss is... Contact: Phone: Location:
Death Row Victim Relatives		Notes: interview death penalty victim...April 19th... available that night or the 20...her daughter abducted from winn dixie and killed..victims rights week..call wendy at atty generals office Contact: Phone: Location:
fl college student of the year		Notes: the fl college student of the year award will be announced sometime today...we have a student in the hunt Contact: Phone: Location: tba?
FSU INTRAMURALS		Notes: A 2 INNING CELEBRATION SOFTBALL GAME FEATURING FSU STUDENTS, FACULTY, AND STAFF, TO MARK THE OPENING OF THE NEW I-M FIELDS....PRESIDENT DALEMBERTE WILL BE ON HAND Contact: Phone: Location: WOODWARD AVE AND ST AUGUSTINE ROAD
harambee festival		Notes: an extravaganza of african..african american and caribbean art in history in the southeast.. mostly a weekend event..might be a stretch to preview..but it could be done Contact: Phone: Location: april 17-19/tallahassee leon-co civic center
hearts aglo must go		Notes: once again our story of some elderly parents who must sell their daughters biz because she amassed huge debts in a severe illness... Contact: Phone: Location: the biz will close on the 22nd
NABORS/plummer		Notes: NABORS NEEDS GEAR..he will be joined by mike plummer who is apparently thinking he will do some sort of promo work,... Contact: Phone: Location:

FIG. 6.2. This is an assignment list, generated by the assignment editor at WTXL-TV in Tallahassee, Florida, using a newsroom computer system. Courtesy of WTXL-TV.

(continued on next page)

Newsroom computer software can be set up to keep track of all these entries and then deliver them as lists, by date.

The list of items for the day becomes the agenda for the morning meeting. Decisions are made as to whether or not to follow up, and what resources to allocate to each story. The list of likely stories becomes the core of the assignment desk list for the day, and the starting point for preparing rundowns at the producers' desks.

Story/Date/Time	Resources	Details
severe wx experts		Notes: couldn't help but notice that nbc news had a nice piece last night on severe storms and tornados with a local expert who had some great graphics from tallahassee..any chance we might consider tracking him down and doing a story...
		at the same time..the board of regents is ready on this date to do a contract with a computer services company on a program that will do comprehensive modeling of hurricane and tropical storm hazards in the state of florida ... Contact: Phone: Location:
SPORTS LIVE?		Notes: SPORTS WANTS TO GO LIVE AT FSU BASEBALL...IT'S FINAL HOME SERIES OF YEAR Contact: Phone: Location: DICK HOWSER STADIUM
fl boating advisory council 8:30:00 AM		Notes: boating safety education..1997 boating safety stats..and the new boating accident report and other boating issues will be explored Contact: Phone: Location: from 8;30-5pm...at the dep building 2600 blair stone rd twin towers building..room 609
MYRA DOES SERIES SHOOT 10:00:00 AM		Notes: MYRA SAYS SHE NEEDS A PHOTOG TO GO DO SOME SERIES WORK TODAY..HOW MUCH OF THE DAY WILL BE DOMINATED BY THIS SHOOT IS UNKNOWN...SHE IS REQUESTING EITHER SUSAN OR ROB Contact: Phone: Location:
red kangaroos 10:00:00 AM		Notes: from 10-'til 12-noon special photo op for the three red male kangas that will be exhibited at the zoo Contact: Phone: Location: talley museum of history and natural science
tpd party patrol 7:00:00 PM		Notes: TALLEY POLICE ARE USING A PARTY PATROL ..A SPECIAL GROUP OF OFFICERS WHO BUST UP PARTIES ON FRIDAY AND SATURDAY NIGHTS AT THIS TIME OF YEAR... Contact: Phone: Location: call tpd to arrange a ride along. sgt. david hendry is a potential contact

FIG. 6.2. (*continued*)

Ongoing Stories

The assignment desk is responsible for checking on stories that occurred in the recent past, especially the day before, and then assessing their newsworthyness for the current day. In a local station the desk has to stay on top of ongoing stories.

Here is an example of what can happen if the desk doesn't keep track of ongoing stories. Two small market stations covered the crash of an advertising blimp late the previous afternoon. The aircraft deflated, and no one was hurt, but its airbag was caught in some trees. It had already been determined that the blimp needed to be extracted from the trees and then taken somewhere for an inspection to see if it could be repaired. One station checked on the status of the blimp story and ran what amounted to a rehash on the 11 p.m. news, although it had telephoned the hospital and ascertained that neither pilot was hospitalized. The next morning, at 9:15, key staff members discussed how to cover the story during the morning meeting. Meanwhile, the competition had called the sheriff's department and the airport manager early in the morning and dispatched a crew to the scene at first light. They had the whole recovery operation on tape when their competitors arrived—just in time to see a flat bed trailer truck pulling out with the damaged aircraft.

The ideal situation is for the Assignment Editor to be able to brief the morning meeting participants on the status and prospects for an ongoing story. This requires at least a few telephone calls first thing in the morning.

Future News

Assembling information on upcoming stories is first and foremost an exercise in meticulous record keeping, as well as having a set routine for reviewing sources that list these events.

A well run news operation continually encourages organizations to mail, fax, or e-mail information and should periodically remind public relations staffs to send news releases. This is an ongoing process due to turnover in the PR offices and the large number of volunteers who manage public events. Sometimes the volunteers are very savvy about media relations, other times they are naive.

There should be regular on-air reminder announcements. Many stations provide a free cellular telephone number that can be used to call in spot news.

One routine that is frequently overlooked is to find out what items on civic board agendas have been held over, or scheduled for further consideration. This means debriefing reporters and making calls to the appropriate offices. Some government units attach lists of future meetings to the current agenda. Others only list their meetings in the legal notices section of a local newspaper.

The assignment desk staff should read the newspapers carefully, it is not unusual for the information you need to be buried several paragraphs down in a story. The desk should routinely request agendas from elected bodies, so that reporters and producers can make an estimate of the newsworthyness of the upcoming meeting. Sharp assignment editors create an *anniversary* file. This leads to stories about the big flood 5 years ago and to historical tie-ins to current events.

Public Safety

One of the jobs that some people working in newsrooms do not like involves doing the *telephone beat*. Local news organizations have a list of agencies that they call one or more times a day to find out if anything newsworthy has happened. These frequently include local police agencies (meaning at least municipal police), sheriff's offices, and the state police or highway patrol. These calls are designed to dig out major events, usually fatality auto accidents and criminal activities. Fire departments are called to determine if any major fires have occurred. Some civic offices may be included on the list. Some hospitals are cooperative, and designate someone to call. Hospitals, however, are far from consistent in their press relations.

THE ASSIGNMENT DESK

There is an art to developing rapport on the telephone. Your objective is to put the person answering the phone at ease, and create an atmosphere that makes them comfortable answering questions and providing information. Listen carefully, don't be "flip" or "phony," and try to sense whether the person answering is busy and harassed. If you read a note in the paper indicating that person was given a reward for meritorious service, be sure to congratulate them. Above all, remember the 5 W's and one H: Who, What, Where, When, Why, and How. Get the facts, and don't be ashamed to call back if you need to clarify something. Be sure you understand what the person who answered is saying, medical and public safety organizations have their own professional jargon.

Some stations maintain networks of *stringers,* part-time reporters who earn a small fee for providing news stories or tips. Never underestimate a stringer. We recall trying to get news out of a particularly antipress sheriff in Kansas. One day we called the stringer, who gave us a rather detailed story about a local crime. We inquired how she had gotten the information. "The sheriff's my brother-in-law," she said.

There may be many other locations to call, depending on the area and local custom. A record should be kept of these names, locations, and telephone numbers. Assignment desk staffs change like other staff, but the resource material should always be available in the computer and on paper.

FIG. 6.3. The assignment editor just looked up a contact on the newsroom computer system and now he is making the call. Photo by P. Keirstead.

Doing the beat calls is an art. The caller tries to establish the confidence of the person who is being called, and over time, tries to promote a friendly, cooperative relationship. Some of the people you call will be friendly, most will be very busy, and some will be grumpy. Keep a smile in your voice, no matter what the reaction on the other end. You will call some agencies regularly, only to be told they have nothing to report. Persistence pays off, keep calling even when they have nothing to say.

Be alert to changes in contact names or numbers, and make certain the information is shared with the appropriate staff members, and most important, record the information in the permanent directory which is part of your newsroom computer system's assignment desk function.

In addition to making beat calls, news departments monitor the radio transmissions of public safety agencies. (The exception is very large cities, where a local press agency does this or where the police send information by data link.)

There are certain legal aspects to monitoring public service agencies that must be observed. The news department should have on file a letter from each agency authorizing the monitoring. Some states have laws that make all public safety monitoring illegal, unless the prohibition is waived by permission.

There is a further complication. FCC rules prohibit rebroadcast of another broadcast station's transmissions without the originator's permission. Using information heard on a public service radio would, technically, be retransmission. People who violate these rules face fines and possible imprisonment on federal charges.

The most important rule: Do not broadcast any information obtained solely from monitoring a public safety agency. You must call that agency and confirm the information, or send a videographer or reporter to the scene. Rebroadcasting the information without the agency's knowledge violates federal law. It also opens the station to law suits if the information is inaccurate.

Listening to public safety broadcasts takes some practice. Most stations use scanners that seek out active transmissions, which means the receiver bounces from frequency to frequency. In order to monitor a scanner, one must learn the voices and style of dispatchers. When a major activity is transmitted, you can lock the scanner on the agency's frequency, once you establish whose transmission you heard. Public safety agencies have been moving toward using scrambling technology on their frequencies, some of which can be descrambled with special receivers, but should not be monitored without the knowledge of the agency. Many police agencies have secure frequencies that cannot be monitored with commercially available civilian technology, so there can be gaps in what is heard in the newsroom.

Almost all public service dispatching is done using codes for types of assignments or activities to speed up the process, cut down on interference by the public, and make the transmissions understandable. Some agencies use a version of the "10-code" in which a 10 is said before the key number. You probably know that "10-4" means, "yes, I heard you and understand." Fire departments and some police agencies use a "signal" code. A fire dispatcher might say: "engine 4, ladder 2, signal 5 at 114 Cross Street." Signal 5 indicates the type of activity reported. Some police agencies use "10" and "signal codes," the signal code tells the receiving officer

THE ASSIGNMENT DESK

what type of incident is being investigated. When the officer radios in a "signal" it tells the dispatcher what action was taken.

Assignment desks will have copies of the local public safety codes. The trick is to learn which calls are likely to lead to a spot news story. After a while, you will become accustomed to listening to the noise of monitors in the background, but only the critical ones will hit your consciousness.

In New York City, a "10-13" means "officer in trouble" and everybody scrambles. A plain English call "shots fired" or "officer down" gets the same reaction. In New York City, a call for "emergency services," which is the specialized police rescue division, bares investigation. Some police agencies inform units of a fire call using a "10-70" code. Many agencies used numbers in a series to indicate vehicular accidents and their severity.

Some fire departments classify the seriousness of fires by the number of alarms issued. You have probably heard of a "four-alarm" fire, which is always serious. One trick when listening to fire dispatchers is to learn the degree of response that is normal in your area for certain types of calls. For example, does the fire department routinely dispatch rescue units, or do they only roll for something serious? In some communities, the majority of fire fighters are also certified emergency medical technicians, and so they roll on medical emergencies that are not of themselves news stories.

The dispatch center in Lincoln County, Maine frequently sends a rescue truck from a local fire department to traffic accidents. The firefighters help the police and emergency medical technicians by cutting battery cables to prevent fires, hosing down fuel spills and standing by with fire extinguishers in case a damaged vehicle ignites. They also provide the "jaws of life" equipment used to help extract victims from seriously damaged vehicles. Due to the small size of local police departments, the volunteer firefighters sometimes help direct traffic at an accident scene. It is frequently difficult to ascertain the seriousness of a traffic accident because the rescue truck responds to such a wide variety of incidents.

Dispatching a *hazchem* truck should get your attention, it's a special hazardous materials unit, designed to deal with toxic and flammable substances. Ladder trucks tend to go to building fires. Foam trucks are used at chemical and fuel fires and at airports.

Of course location is important in following fire calls. An alarm at a college is going to get several engines, the police, and probably an emergency medical unit, solely because of the nature of the buildings and the high concentration of people in the area.

Predicting Potential News Stories

There is a "crystal ball" aspect to assignment desk work. Some news organizations place so much emphasis on looking forward, they actually have a planning desk within the assignment operation.

A classic example of planning is preparing for elections. A great deal of information has to be gathered, such as accurate lists of candidates, and their party affiliation, for each office in each jurisdiction that is holding an election. You need to know some of the election ground rules, for example, are elections nonpartisan, how long does the official serve, and what constitutes being elected? In Florida, for example, you win an election when you get 50% plus one vote.

Photos and biographies of candidates also will be needed. It is necessary to find out when the polls will open and close and where the votes are counted in each jurisdiction.

Briefing documents need to be created that contain biographical information about the candidates, a summary of their public policy statements, and any historical or related information about the particular office or race.

Logistics must be addressed. How do you get the results from each jurisdiction? Is there is a way to obtain results from government computers? Do you need to hire poll watchers to gather results? How are you going to handle the reporting of the results? What remotes will be needed? How will the vote totals be assembled in the newsroom? Where will the winning candidates be located once the vote is counted?

There are several election software packages available, including some that are sold by the firms that install newsroom computer systems. Each program requires that certain information be entered into the computer in order for the software to do its job. Another computer-related concern is preprogramming the character generator with a standard screen layout for election statistics. All the races and candidates have to be listed and then double- and triple-checked for spelling, party affiliation, and candidate dropouts.

Most major public events require considerable advance planning and a lot of consultation with other departments. For example, the annual Rose Festival parade is of as much concern to the public affairs department, promotion, and engineering, as it is to the news department. All these departments play major roles in this type of event, especially if the TV or cable station is originating live coverage of the event.

Good news planning departments try to spot trends. Frequently this is done by reading literature others may not read. For example, business periodicals frequently point out trends that have broad effects on the community. University research publications may point out water quality concerns. Church publications may address issues such as changes in the formality of church services or reveal new programs churches are offering in the community. Health trends make interesting news, as do sports and recreational pursuits. Growth in a community can turn into a very hot political topic. Digging around in those thick, technical reports that state and local governments publish can lead to revealing findings.

Following weather trends not only generates interesting stories on its own, it may lead to predictors that affect agriculture and tourism. Population studies frequently indicate important trends for government. For example, one state discovered that it might have an additional 100,000 students seeking to attend public colleges in a relatively short span of time. The planning unit or assignment desk should know the e-mail addresses of census data sites.

THE ASSIGNMENT DESK

Tie-Ins to Other News Stories

One sign of a good Assignment Editor is the person's ability to take a heavily reported international or national story and find a local angle. Let's say there have been several stories on the network recently having to do with poor relations between India and Pakistan. The assignment desk might start looking for someone who is expert on the area. Logical starting points would be local universities, where you might discover experts on the area or the issues. By inquiring in the churches, temples, and mosques of the religious community or calling leaders of ethnic communities, the desk might discover someone who came from these countries. The result might be a local feature that could tie in to this international story.

The faculty members might be able to elaborate on the political and historical reasons for the conflict. Someone from a religious or ethnic community might be involved in sending aid to the area and can probably refer you to natives of the area who live in your community.

Medical stories emanate from the *New England Journal of Medicine* on a regular basis. If there were a medical school or major medical center in your community, the assignment desk could come up with someone who could interpret a medical finding reported in the *Journal*.

Anytime the network does a story about an activity that also takes place in your community, there is a potential tie-in. A network feature on adult learning could easily be supplemented with local material about GED programs (high school equivalency) or adult literacy or migrant literacy programs.

The desk should not overlook retirees, who frequently have a great deal of knowledge about a topic in the news. The Retired Officers Association and local units of the National Guard and the military reserve frequently include people who have been involved in activities that come up in news stories. For example, a U.S. Marine barracks was attacked by terrorists in Beirut, Lebanon in the 1980s. There may be a survivor of that event living in your community.

Idea Clearinghouse

Writers, reporters, editors, producers, and managers with ideas can send messages to the desk, where the bits and pieces can be compiled, distributed, and followed up. The computer system encourages greater participation because it is easy to keyboard a note and send it to the assignment desk.

Here is an example of a story that nearly didn't get done: A station in a medium-sized city is located on the same major street as a "national-brand" motel that always filled up for football weekends, homecoming and graduation. One day it was apparent that something was wrong at the motel because there were no cars parked there and the place looked messy. It took the station 2 weeks to find out the motel's owners had gone out of business. The information was discovered when the bankruptcy documents were filed. Undoubtedly at least a dozen employees passed that spot, but no one alerted the assignment desk. It is imperative that a news organization train everyone, including the staffs other departments, to act as spotters and report any detail, even if the person reporting it is not sure how important it is.

Good stories on bad intersections have been done because a neighbor complained to someone who worked for a TV station, and that person mentioned it to the assignment desk, where it was researched on the telephone, and a videographer was asked to drive by and take at look.

How was it researched? A desk assistant called the traffic division of the police department and determined how many collisions had occurred at the intersection in the previous 12 months. Then, the desk assistant called the president of the neighborhood association, who confirmed the problem and suggested other neighbors who could be called for eyewitness accounts of accidents that had taken place. The desk assistant backed up this information with a call to the city traffic engineer, who admitted there had been problems at that location.

News executives can throw out ideas at any time of day or night by e-mailing the desk. The same goes for producers.

Monitoring Politics

A news organization's reporters should be talking with their contacts frequently, but the Assignment Editor can contribute a great deal by calling a handful of contacts any time the tempo slows down. It never hurts to talk with the public relations person at the local political party headquarters or chat with an incumbent or potential candidate. Those conversations can yield ideas for a story, and they raise the familiarity level, which is important when the crunch of election campaigning begins.

The same approach can be used with organizations that play background roles in local politics. In one community in the southeast, the political power emanates from the neighborhood homeowners' associations, and their "umbrella" organization that represents all the neighborhood groups. The leaders of these organizations are frequently well informed about what is going on below the surface of local government and politics.

There are key individuals in the community who like to know what is happening in the political world. Their insights are frequently useful. This type of person may not call in with a story, but a sharp journalist can develop a story based on what the source has to say about local politics. Union officials are good sources for stories having to do with industry, large medical centers and the public schools.

Trolling "Fringe" Areas

One of the real problems in TV news is covering the less populated suburbs and smaller communities outside the center city. Most television news departments simply do not have sufficient staff to assign people daily to these areas, especially in smaller markets with widely scattered rural communities.

THE ASSIGNMENT DESK

There are some strategies that work. They are highly dependent on meticulous record keeping on the computer system, and setting up a good e-mail network. One of the best systems is to set up a network of *informants*, people, usually with some journalism training, who call, fax, or e-mail minor items that can be included in broadcasts as anchor copy (readers) or dropped into the future file for action later on. This network should be backed up by a system of regular beat calls to public officials (town clerks, county managers, etc.) as well as political leaders. Sometimes it is possible to work out an arrangement with a local radio station or a weekly newspaper, whereby they keep you informed about local news and are available to assist your reporters when you send out a crew.

The newsroom should take subscriptions to as many suburban or rural newspapers as possible. They are good for highlighting on-going local issues and providing information for future coverage. Many of these publications publish weekly e-mail news summaries that provide links to the full text of the week's top stories. Assignment editors should subscribe to these free e-mailings, and check them promptly when they arrive. Some assignment editors set up a regular system for checking Web sites of nearby newspapers and broadcast stations.

A news department should give out its e-mail address frequently via on-air promotions, anchor mentions, and staff business cards. The station should circulate the address and contact numbers for public affairs notices, and have someone screen them for feature ideas.

Although it is difficult to give rural areas the coverage they deserve, think in terms of stories that might affect similar areas, such as building a town water system, or dealing with crop damage. One station in the Midwest lined up a list of events taking place in small towns, and sent a videographer out on Saturday to shoot some VO tape and pick up any information available. The tape was used for weekend news broadcasts, either as short stories, or as a single piece with the video edited as a package. Most important of all: Make certain those beat calls are done regularly!

Monitoring the Pulse of the Market

One practical problem facing almost all local broadcast news organizations is that they can seldom match the level of staffing at the local daily newspaper. The best way to tap into sources is to spend some time in the centers of activity, such as city hall, every day.

Some broadcast stations have sufficient staff to assign fairly narrow beats to reporters, such as city government or the schools. This puts eyes and ears out in the community. Lacking these sources, the assignment desk has to promote good relations during beat phone calls.

The station should keep up-to-date records listing the public relations representatives of local organizations, including the municipal and county government, businesses, colleges and universities, civic organizations, hospitals, the Chamber of Commerce, and public relations agencies.

FINDING PEOPLE

One of the strengths of a well-run assignment desk is having an outstanding database of telephone, fax, and e-mail information. The list starts with the newsroom staff. It is essential to be able to reach staff members when a schedule change is necessary or a crisis erupts. Personnel changes frequently in many broadcast news departments, so the job of keeping the list has to be assigned to someone who meticulously keeps it up to date.

Once the staff directory is completed, the next project is to set up an easy-to-access database of frequent contacts. This is where the assignment desk does the equivalent of acquiring all the little slips of paper and "sticky tabs" on which people have written contact numbers. One important element to this effort is to train the staff to message the desk anytime they acquire a new telephone number that would be useful.

Frequently dialed numbers should be set up for speed dialing. This includes public safety dispatchers, key police and fire personnel, municipal and county leaders, and some political sources. Many stations develop special contact files for use when an emergency develops. Let's say a serious forest fire breaks out. By going to that file, the assignment editor on duty has an instant guide that indicates who to call at what agencies.

Today's communication systems require that we get a variety of numbers: not only regular (landline) telephone numbers, but numbers for cellular telephones, pagers, fax machines, and e-mail addresses. Experienced reporters try to acquire as many direct line or private line numbers as possible, so that they do not have to deal with operators, receptionists, and automated telephone systems. One old trick is to read the numbers on desk telephones of sources.

Cross-indexing is important, especially for people who are not called frequently. It's not unusual to hear a producer inquire if anyone knows the number of the speech pathologist interviewed last month.

A new executive producer at WTXL-TV in Tallahassee, Florida showed real initiative during a routine call to a local airport. The only number on file was the airport administrator's office. The executive producer outlasted the recorded greeting and reached someone in the office. After asking a couple of questions, the producer asked for the number for the Federal Aviation Administration tower (where the air traffic controllers are stationed). Once he got to speak to someone with the FAA, the producer talked the official into providing the 24-hour direct phone number, so that the station could obtain information quickly in event of an airport crisis.

How can a new news operation build a telephone number database? First, have someone go through the government listings in the telephone directory and copy the numbers you think might be useful. Then follow up by calling and trying to obtain useful numbers that are not always shared with the public. Examples would include the police detective bureau and the coroner's mobile and home numbers. How about administrative, 24-hour-a-day numbers at the county jail? Get private numbers of political leaders, such as members of the county commission. Do you have direct numbers for each fire station? How about volunteer fire companies, do you have the home and work numbers of the fire chief? Check the local Web sites of government entities, they frequently list all the telephone numbers.

When you get a number from a person, send a business card or some other mailer with all the station news number on it to each contact. This way, they can call you, or return a call to you.

Local colleges and universities are excellent sources for information, people to interview, features, and sports information. Some schools compile contact lists so that if you need to find an expert on Mongolia's natural resources, you simply turn to the school's source directory. If possible, this directory should be put into the department's computer database.

Associations and nonprofit charitable groups make good sources. There is an association to represent almost any interest you can name. These organizations tend to cluster in state capitals and the national capital, but not always. These groups can quickly provide background information and point out people who you might want to interview. Most communities have a Chamber of Commerce that will be tapped into business and economic concerns. Many communities have a Better Business Bureau that will help with consumer issues.

Again, don't forget the Internet, where use of a search engine will produce information about many associations dealing with social issues. There is virtually no limit to the sources you can dredge up. There more of this information that can be posted to a database in a logical, easy-to-find way, the better off you will be when a story breaks.

News organizations spend quite a bit of money for technology to keep their staffs in contact. Pagers and cellular telephones make communicating easy. Many businesses and offices are hesitant to let you use their phones.

Bureaus are frequently equipped with fax machines as well as a connection to the newsroom computer system. A bureau should have an answering machine or voice mail. Some staff members should have personal voice mail.

Staff members should be reminded to silence their pagers and cellular telephones in some situations, such as when they are attending a news conference or at a hostage situation.

Some TV stations rely on private two-way radio systems for communication between the base and mobile units. The most sophisticated versions use scrambling technology to avoid having their messages intercepted by someone with a scanner. There are protocols to be observed when using two-way radio equipment. The FCC regulations are fairly simple, but must be observed.

Large news organizations can purchase databases of telephone numbers or Internet database services, which are much more convenient than keeping shelves of telephone books, or relying on directory assistance services.

ISSUING ASSIGNMENTS

The newsroom computer system plays a major role in issuing assignments. It is possible to have the day's list of assignments programmed to generate forms that supply the relevant information to a crew. During the workday, two major responsibilities of the assignment desk are to develop assignments and keep track of who is doing what in regard to the assignments, and who will need to be relieved by a fresh staff member during long drawn-out coverage.

Developing Assignments

The assignment desk first compiles a list of all potential assignments, those on file, carry-overs from earlier breaking items, features, requests. These are discussed during the morning meeting. The producers quickly focus in on the items that they feel have the greatest potential of being included in their broadcasts, the assignment editor and the operations director discuss logistics issues, and then the assignment desk issues any assignments that have not already been given out. Some assignments will have already been issued because they are part of ongoing coverage or because a crew had to be in place early in the day.

The assignment desk and the producers must work together but the assignment desk has the responsibility to keep track of everyone and everything. Producers must make certain they inform the assignment desk if they make requests that affect other news coverage or the plans of other producers.

The term *crew* can mean many things. In a small market television or cable news operation, the "crew" could be one person, who reports and shoots the tape, including the interviews. In many markets, a crew is two people, the reporter and the videographer/technician, who may also operate an ENG or SNV truck. At the other extreme, a network crew might include a correspondent, a field producer, a videographer, a sound operator, a lighting technician, and a *grip*. A grip is a crew member who does anything the other technicians don't do. In a studio, a grip would set up and take down scenery.

Just how much the assignment desk does in preparing for each assignment differs with the story and who is assigned to it. For the sake of picking an example, assume that the desk has developed a story involving putting the last beam in place during the construction of a major bridge. This is the sort of event that the assignment desk would give to a general assignment reporter, who is then teamed with the next available videographer. The assignment sheet would give the time the crew has to be there, the location, a description of what is happening, and who is participating, who to contact at the location, a list of special requirements, a target time to complete the assignment, a copy of a press release, and which broadcast needs the main story, as well as any other broadcasts that may want a version of the story.

The bare bones of the assignment form would be recorded on the assignment log for the day, so producers can inquire how the story is developing. It is the responsibility of the crew to keep the desk informed how the work is progressing, and the assignment desk is expected to check if the crew doesn't call in regularly.

The assignment desk also tracks material coming in on feeds, or being delivered via messenger. All of this information is typed into the computer system so that status reports can be called up at any point by the producers or management.

THE ASSIGNMENT DESK 105

The work of the assignment desk is not static. While it is overseeing current coverage, it is developing future stories, and listening and watching for breaking news. Most crews do two or more assignments per day, so it is important that the desk know where a crew is at every moment, and frequently the desk is called on to juggle arrangements if a crew experiences a delay or an equipment problem. In large metropolitan news operations, the assignment desk may dispatch messengers to pick up tape and bring it back for editing. Crew members usually carry pagers and cellphones to make it possible for the assignment desk or a producer to locate specific crew members.

THE FEED DESK

Medium and larger market news organizations frequently designate one or more persons to keep track of feeds from the affiliate news service, syndicators, and cooperatives. Feeds may come via satellite, special fiber optic telephone circuits, or over the Internet. Much of the process can be automated. The schedule and satellite coordinates, fiber optic circuit, or Internet information are entered into a computer database that triggers recording devices, tape or disk, at the designated time.

Generally the feeds are accumulated in one storage location, and then copies are made of the pieces or coverage that producers say they wish to use. It is possible, using computer technology, to network the video from the storage tape or disk into a specific edit suite or to a writer's or producer's desktop computer.

Supporting lists of offerings, with cues and (sometimes) scripts, are provided directly to the newsroom computer system through several data delivery services. One job the feed coordinator must do is to keep track of special feeds, which may come in at other than regular feed times.

The feed coordinator may be responsible for handling outgoing feeds. For example, Florida News Network members feed their offering to one receiving station, which then makes up a master reel with all the offerings, prepares a list with cues and relevant information, and at a preset time, transmits the reel of offerings via satellite to the member stations. Another situation that arises frequently requires that the feed coordinator lease time by calling a company that sells "occasional time" on satellites and arrange for an outgoing feed, either to the network, or to another news organization that has requested material. All of this is reported to and coordinated by the assignment desk.

RESEARCH: SEARCHING THE WEB

Many news operations place a PC with Internet access in the assignment desk area. It is necessary to have some control over who uses the Internet, so one reasonable solution is to place a general newsroom terminal in the assignment desk area where there is both access and supervision. Assignment desk personnel find the Internet very helpful in terms of looking up background information, finding contacts and telephone numbers, searching for supporting stories, checking

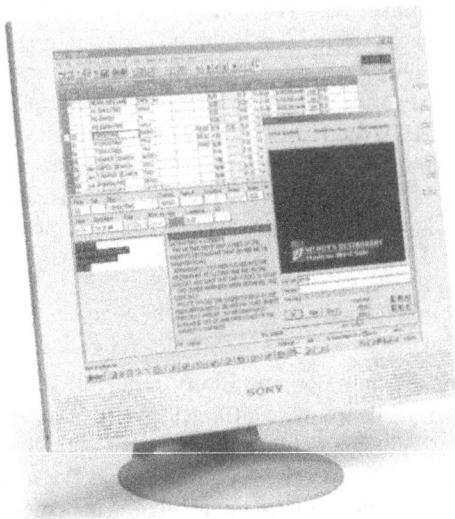

FIG. 6.5. A Sony monitor shows an Avid iNews producer rundown. The square on the right side of the monitor can be used to import video. © 2004 Avid Technology, Inc. All rights reserved. Avid is a registered trademark or trademark of Avid Technology, Inc., in the United States and/or other countries. Photo is provided courtesy of Avid Technology, Inc.

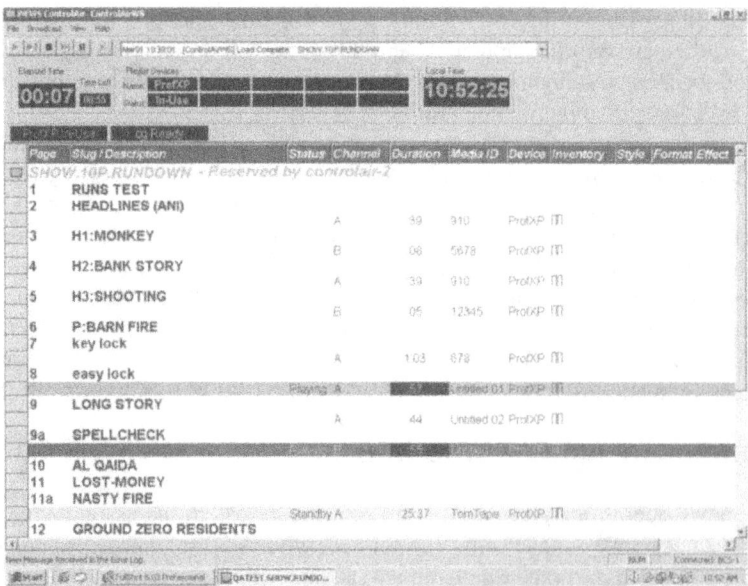

FIG. 6.6. A closer view of a producer rundown from an Avid iNews newsroom automation system. © 2004 Avid Technology, Inc. All rights reserved. Avid is a registered trademark or trademark of Avid Technology, Inc., in the United States and/or other countries. Photo is provided courtesy of Avid Technology, Inc.

weather forecasts, or finding maps. Some cues, scripts, and even feeds are e-mailed to stations. Producers at WTVT in Tampa, Florida frequently drop by the assignment desk to research stories. A detailed discussion of Internet utilization is found in chapter 9 (this volume).

THE BREAKING STORY, PREPARING FOR THE CRUNCH

The assignment desk hits its stride when a major story breaks. Usually, the desk is the first to know because the first word of a spot story usually comes as the result of a telephone call from a staff member, the public, the public safety monitors, or is on the wire service.

No matter how first word arrives, there are two actions to be taken. First, the assignment desk must alert producers and the executive producer there may be a breaking story, and second, confirm it. Once confirmed, most news operations want senior news executives notified, and may routinely notify other departments, especially engineering.

Accuracy and speed are the key words when a story breaks. One press agency used to like to say it wanted to be "first … and right." It was a tongue-in-cheek retort to another agency that prided itself in being first in delivering breaking stories to subscribers.

Of course, the nature of a breaking story affects the way coverage is carried out. The crash of a commercial aircraft gets one type of coverage, the resignation of the mayor gets another.

The newsroom computer can play a make-or-break role in breaking news coverage. Some news operations even have special scenario files on their system. If you enter *aviation crash* in a designated screen, the computer instantly displays a prioritized list of actions to be taken and phone calls to be made, with the relevant telephone, beeper, cellular telephone numbers, and contact names.

What are the priorities?

1. Confirmation and early details. Informing key personnel.
2. Getting a crew or crews to the scene.
3. Informing newsroom supervisors, discussing bulletin or special coverage, or changes to an upcoming broadcast.
4. Staffing and notification.
5. Major logistics.

What, exactly, has to be done in each step? Let's assume that a commercial jet airliner crashes just after takeoff from your city's major airport:

Confirmation

There is no point in raising everyone's respiration rate until you have a confirmed story. Let's say you picked up your first tip from the public safety monitor:

Clear all traffic ... all channels: Airport one and two, engine 12, ladder 6, engine 8, engine 11, engine 27, battalion chief west, rescue one, rescue three, hazchem—aircraft fire—228th Street and Corning Boulevard ... repeat....

First call: (Use the automatic dialer) the Fire department public affairs office (the dispatchers will be too busy). Second call: Federal Aviation Administration tower. Turn up FAA monitor ... tower is holding all aircraft due to "emergency."

Other confirmation: police dispatcher sending several units to the area. The call is "assist fire department—code 3 (lights and siren permitted). Check ambulance frequency: also dispatching.

Viewers (3) call on cellphone number, report a big noise like an explosion near Corning Boulevard and 228th Street. One says he saw a big plane dive toward earth, followed by explosion (get name and number for eyewitness report).

Dial station public address system through telephone, "Your attention please, this is the assignment desk, all news staff members to the newsroom, we have a report of an aircraft accident."

Crews to Scene

You can't shoot video until you get a videographer there, so send the nearest videographer and a live truck, even if you have to pull the crew off another assignment. If the first unit to get there is a videographer in a company car, move at least one live unit into the area so that you will be able to transmit both live cut-ins and live reports for the upcoming broadcasts.

A desk assistant will get on the Internet, or use installed map software, and retrieve a map of the crash location to be used to guide units going to the scene, and as an illustration for on-air coverage.

Notify the helicopter service. Most stations lease helicopters, so if the chopper isn't in the air, get it airborne. (The helicopter pilot should try to get live aerial shots but may have to pull back to clear for police and air rescue traffic.) Ask engineering or the operations producer to increase the staff in the taping area, as you will want to tape everything coming in from the microwave trucks and helicopter. Send another crew to the scene and a crew and microwave truck to the airport. You will dispatch more crews in a few minutes.

Inform

Using whatever method works best (telephone, loud voice, conference call), brief the news director, executive producer, operations producer and all line producers on duty. If a major executive is not present, have them paged or called on their cellphones. Tell everyone what you know, what you have done. Most general managers want to be informed of a breaking story of this magnitude.

The group will decide on a quick coverage strategy. In most cases, the senior news executive present: news director, executive producer, senior producer, will take charge of coverage at this point, freeing the assignment desk to handle specific tasks.

The first major decision will be: Do we go live? The likely answer is going to be "yes," if a live unit can get close enough to get at least a cover shot of the crash scene. The executive producer will probably designate a producer to handle all live coverage, so the scheduled broadcast producers can continue to work on their programs. An anchor is assigned. Engineering and production will staff the news control room. Because commercial and program production is underway in the studios, the anchor will use a newsroom location for the live coverage. Some stations have a fixed camera installed in the newsroom so that there is always a place available to anchor live coverage. Engineering will need to be involved because there may be special demands on the facilities including turning on special lighting in the newsroom.

The news director informs the general manager and alerts sales, traffic, and programming because commercials for airlines must be canceled, and others will have to be moved or made up later. The news promotion specialist is also alerted because additional promotional announcements may be needed, and existing announcements will have to be revised or replaced.

The microwave truck has found a location that is slightly elevated from the crash scene, and yet not close enough to cause problems for rescue personnel and investigators. You have live pictures and a reporter. A videographer is roaming, trying to pick up closer video in the area. The video will be fed from the truck. The helicopter pilot managed to tape some aerial shots but has to clear the area for emergency traffic. The chopper feed has been taped. A field producer and a tape editor are en route to the microwave truck.

The helicopter may be able to do electronic relays for you if the microwave truck is having trouble getting a good signal back to the studios. The helicopter can deliver tape, but this is risky in bad weather, CBS News once lost a correspondent, a pilot, the helicopter, and the newsfilm when the aircraft crashed taking-off in a severe storm to relay film from Pennsylvania to New York.

The reporter assigned to the microwave truck radios that she now has enough information to do a cut-in. The crash producer notifies master control, they agree on a switch from regular programming to the bulletin and live feed in 35 seconds. The lights are turned on at the anchor position. An associate producer hands the anchor some opening copy. "And ... 5 ... 4 ... 3 ... 2 ... 1 ... we're live." The cut-in starts with the crash scene reporter standing so the rescue activity can be seen. The video switches to the aerial tape shot by the helicopter, and the crash reporter tosses the feed to the airport reporter, who is able to give details on which airline and flight is involved. An associate producer in the studio finishes an Internet search, and types a quick information note telling the crash producer the type, age, and safety record of the downed aircraft. The crash reporter takes the feed back, does a quick live interview with an eyewitness, and concludes with information about the plane and a recap of what is known to the moment. If weather has been a factor, you may need to cut to the station weather office for comments from your meteorologist.

Staffing

The next move, which involves the assignment desk and the executive producer, is to determine what other locations need to be covered, such as hospitals or a temporary morgue. Crews will need to be dispatched to stand by at locations that may be related to the main story. The executive producer may want another crew to shoot several interviews with eyewitnesses. If the airline chooses a temporary headquarters location other than the airport, it will have to be covered.

It is also necessary to account for loss of light as night approaches and to set up relief crews for the crash scene and airport coverage, which is likely to continue for 3 or 4 days.

An associate producer may be assigned to research, building a file on the history of the airline and the type of aircraft involved, as well as the safety record of the local airport. There probably will be other sidebar (related) stories having to do with property damage, injuries, fatalities on the ground, and others about the community's response to a major accident.

While all this is going on, the assignment desk telephone will be ringing constantly. The test of a good assignment editor or producer is being able to be calm and professional during a time of great stress. Calmness is a mark of leadership.

Major Logistics

Although the assignment desk is not always responsible for some of the logistical issues that accompany a major breaking story, the desk needs to be aware of most details. If a microwave truck has an equipment failure, the desk must be aware of the problem and ask engineering to assign a replacement vehicle if one is available. The desk may have to assign someone from forward planning to the daily assignment desk to help with the increased load.

The Assignment Editor will also need to hold back on even discussing some minor story options because they won't be used and the management staff needs to focus on the big story.

The Assignment Editor usually develops sources who may be able to offer special information or insight during a time of crisis. Sometimes one of these sources will lead a news organization to information and therefore, a story, its competitors do not have.

Once the first burst of activity is over during a breaking story, the people and information available to all the media may be fairly similar, which magnifies the need to develop unique stories in a competitive marketplace.

We saved the biggest headache for last. The assignment desk will probably have to provide resources and support to one or more networks. At first, the networks will want satellite or cable feeds of material the station acquired right after the crash. After their crews get on the scene, the support will be in the form of space to write and edit, information and transmission facilities.

All through the process of covering a major breaking story, computers will play a critical role, as research tools, remote writing terminals, remote prompters, and messaging devices, among other functions.

A VISIT TO THE ASSIGNMENT DESK

WTVT-TV, Channel 13, FOX in Tampa, Florida

As you look around the assignment desk area, which takes up almost one wall of the newsroom plus a medium-sized office nearby, you see seven multichannel scanners, two newsroom computer system terminals (one of which has a list of assignments up on the screen), a PC for Internet access, a text pager terminal, and several telephones. The assignment editor is pacing back and forth along the counter that holds terminals and other equipment. A production assistant is working at a terminal on the far end of the desk. A planning editor is working in the office.

The production assistant updates an earlier report that a body had been found near a beach. She says the videographer knows to wait until the body is covered before shooting. She says the authorities think it is a missing member of a shrimp boat crew.

We scan the work area. Posted in plain view is the Fox 13 News hot phone list. There are lots of phones, monitors, and clipboards.

A news staffer goes to the PC to access the Internet in order to do research for a story on Lakeland High School students who may have been plotting to murder their parents. There has been discussion about the youths accessing an Internet site that might have given them the idea. The staff member is trying to find the site.

There is a tray of news releases sitting on the counter, along with lots of phone books and a pile of detailed map books of the Tampa Bay area. (News coverage in Tampa Bay is complicated because the area has two large cities, Tampa and St. Petersburg, plus dozens of populous smaller communities, and the bay provides a natural barrier to efficient driving across the metropolitan area.)

The Assignment Editor says the station will supply pool video from a murder suspect's first appearance for Channel 28 because they have done WTVT a lot of favors. Someone grumbles, but the assignment editor is adamant.

There are several pull down maps along the wall behind the assignment desk.

10:37 a.m. The Tampa fire dispatcher sends units to a daycare center. The assignment editor looks up a number and calls the daycare center, there is no fire.

He used a detailed street atlas. The editor logs the activity on his terminal.

The Assignment Editor calls Unit 18 on the company radio. Many messages to units are typed on a digital pager keyboard located on the assignment desk. WTVT also subscribes to a nationwide pager system that reports major fires around the country. The desk just got a report of a serious fire in Colorado. Why does the station have a pager that alerts the editor to a fire in Colorado? Because the cost is minimal and sometime it tips the deck to a fire in the WTVT coverage area.

The Assignment Editor confers with a producer to determine the type of coverage that is needed of the Florida State Fair, which is underway near Tampa.

FIG. 6.4. An assignment desk assistant editor at WTVT-TV in Tampa is paging a videographer. Photo by P. Keirstead.

The assignment desk is working on:

The Florida State Fair.

The Gasparilla Festival in Tampa.

A presidential news conference to be fed later in the morning.

The Lakeland teen murders.

The body of a missing shrimper that washed up.

The Assignment Editor turns up the fire department monitor. There is a report of a man shot, but it turns out he shot himself on the job with a construction worker's nail gun. The Tampa fire department provides rescue and emergency services.

An assignment editor has to be a storehouse of information. A new editor, producer, or reporter joining a news department has to learn, for starters, how local government is organized, the nature and jurisdictions of police agencies, who runs the ambulance service, and the location of major buildings. WTVT's Assignment Editor has several years' experience in Tampa.

A laser printer is installed at assignment desk. It is connected by a computer network to newsroom terminals. There is also a dot matrix printer is in a sound box in the middle of newsroom, for less critical printing jobs.

THE ASSIGNMENT DESK   113

In between incoming telephone calls, the assignment desk production assistant has been using the archives function on a newsroom terminal to look up information and to answer questions called in by viewers. Most of the work involves checking information in old news stories. (What was the phone number for that spouse abuse hotline?)

NETWORKS

The assignment desk in a network headquarters operates a little differently from the assignment desk at a local station. The primary function of a network assignment desk is to coordinate a deluge of information coming in to the newsroom, and then distribute lists to relevant personnel, on terminal screen, phone, or even, in person.

One list, of course, is a compilation of the stories that are being covered by the network, its affiliates, or its contract news services, such as APTV and Reuters Television. Another is called the "who's where," a list of the location, contact details, and story assignment of reporters, correspondents, crews, and numbers where executives can be located when they are traveling.

The assignment desk constantly monitors the press agency wires. It also makes frequent contact with network bureaus in the United States and overseas. The bureaus regularly advise the desk what stories they are working on, and immediately notify the desk if they hear about a breaking story. The desk also monitors coverage lists provided by its video news services.

Owned and operated stations (stations owned by the network's parent company) and network affiliates are good sources of news tips, and so desk personnel check with many of the larger stations several times a day. The network's own bureaus provide a great deal of input, especially the Washington bureau.

The assignment desk in a traditional network news organization such as CBS News has two functions. It keeps an overview of all newsgathering activities, and it assists individual news broadcasts in keeping track of coverage specifically labeled for each broadcast. This division causes disputes from time to time, especially when the powerful evening news broadcast tries to tie up most of the correspondent resources on a major story.

The network assignment desk also maintains liaison with the organization's own affiliate video service, and its affiliate video exchange. Sometimes stories that are being circulated on a regional basis can be useful to national coverage. One example is a "roundup" story, in which video from several similar situations is combined into one larger story. An example would be flooding over several states. Instead of reporting on each flood, the network would combine all the flood stories into a "roundup."

Network assignment desks are staffed 24 hours a day, 7 days a week. The editors can dispatch correspondents and crews directly, or call a bureau and instruct the bureau to send a crew. Some networks have a special *foreign desk* that specializes in international coverage. This is helpful because there are many considerations, including time, access, and means to transmit a story, which have to be worked out on a foreign story. Sometimes the foreign desk does newsgathering by calling officials overseas in order to determine the nature and significance of a story. The foreign desk also deals with network bureaus overseas and with other news organizations that cooperate by exchanging video.

The foreign desk also keeps track of trends and activities around the world, and advises executive producers and other decision-makers, either by pointing out potential stories or by evaluating an existing situation. In some cases the foreign desk may deal directly with a correspondent or producer who is covering a story overseas. The foreign desk also becomes involved in logistics, ordering satellite circuits, and working out travel or shipping arrangements. A journalist who wants to work on a foreign desk is always in a better position if he or she speaks at least one language other than English.

CONCLUSION

Assignment desk work has the excitement missing from some other jobs in which a person uses a computer terminal most of the day. A journalist who desires to become a news manager should put in some time on the assignment desk in order to learn its techniques, and to understand the problems assignment editors face. The assignment desk is not for everyone, so there can be opportunities on the desk for quick learners who are setting their sights on senior management or producer positions in broadcast journalism. Working at the assignment desk hones your ability to work under pressure, with grace, as well as expanding your knowledge of newsroom computer systems, a skill that will be useful as you move to other posts in the newsroom.

7

Computers in the Control Room

The linking of diverse computers and other hardware called *networking* marked a major step in bringing efficiency and organization to the production of news. It also opened the way for automation of news production. During the late 1980s, links were developed that integrated the broadcast newsroom computer system into other automation systems throughout broadcast facilities. Links were made with the traffic computers for advertising, with engineering computers to play tapes and with billing computers to invoice customers. In this chapter you will see how the various departments interact with news production in a typical TV station. The final section will look at the engineering and production departments because they work in an interdependent manner.

THE TYPICAL STATION

The major departments that are found in television stations are as follows.

Administration (The General Manager's Office)

The overall policy for the station's operation is set in the general manager's office. The general manager reports to group or corporate executives if the station is one of several owned by the same company. In business terms, the general manager has profit and loss responsibility for the organization. Human resources (personnel), telecommunications, building maintenance, and security frequently fall under this department.

Most computer-related functions in the administrative office are confidential. The one part of the General Manager's office computer system that is linked to the rest of the station is the internal network, called an *Intranet,* that is used to carry messages and documents.

Every business has its unique structure, but it is likely that the personnel office will be closely associated with the general manager's office due to its hiring, equal opportunity and human resources responsibilities.

Business Office

The business office is where the billing generated by the sales department is processed, supplies and materials are purchased, payrolls calculated, and all federally regulated business expense is tracked. The business office internal computers have firewalls and are inaccessible to the rest of the station.

Sales

The majority of the station's income is earned through the sale of advertising. Most sales departments are headed by a general sales manager, who frequently oversee separate units dealing with national sales, regional sales, local sales, research and traffic.

The sales department is highly computerized because of the complex process that takes place in selling advertising time. The sales department has to keep track of a vast *inventory* or *availabilities* (available commercial positions) that sell at different prices depending on the audience at the time. Pricing is dependent on the advertiser's requirement that the spots reach a certain estimated number of people (ratings points), the gross number of spots ordered, discounts for volume or frequency, discounts for special sales packages, discounts for permitting spots to preempted by advertisers who will pay more, and negotiated deals made by the sales department.

The sales department is connected by computer to a "representative" organization that represents the station in major ad-buying markets, such as New York, Detroit, Chicago, and Los Angeles. In the trade, these companies area called *Reps.*

Internally, sales persons use computer software to prepare speculative and final schedules for advertisers. They rely, also, on statistical and ratings information developed by the station's in-house research specialist.

When advertising is sold, the relevant information is entered in a traffic system that provides the scheduling unit with information on what commercials to run and when to run them. The same software is used to keep track of the spots to make certain they did run, and make adjustments if they did not run. The sales traffic system also gathers billing information for use by the business department.

Programming

The internal structure of program departments varies quite a bit depending on the degree of authority of the program manager has to purchase programs that run outside of network times. The network with which a station has an affiliation contract provides both "must carry" and optional programming that account for the majority of most stations' airtime.

The program manager has four distinct areas of responsibility. One is to analyze the station's programming, and the competition's programming, and then work with station (and sometimes, corporate) executives to plan a schedule and buy programs to run locally. The second responsibility is to oversee all local production, which includes news, public affairs, and other local programming. The third responsibility is to make certain the station meets its public affairs programming and other public service obligations, and the fourth responsibility is to assure the on-time production of accurate operating logs (schedule of all events for the day).

The program traffic department uses commercial sales information entered in the computer system by the sales traffic department, programming information developed internally and from network messages, and public service and promotional announcements to compile daily operating schedules. These schedules, called *logs*, are second-by-second lists of *events*, meaning programs, commercials, promotional announcements, and public service announcements. There are important business and regulatory rules that must be followed in compiling the log.

The data in the program *log*, or daily schedule, is fed to a computer that directs other computers that actually deliver programming to air. Accuracy is paramount in the program traffic department, because a mistaken entry can cause chaos in an automation system. Mistakes cost money when advertisements don't run as scheduled.

The program log, in the form of computer data, becomes the database that runs the station's automated systems. The log is downloaded into computers that store commercials, promotions, and public service announcements, as well as programs. These systems are dependent on computer systems being able to "talk" to each other and share data.

A program manager may supervise a traffic supervisor, a production manager, a creative director, and in some facilities, the promotion department. The traffic supervisor is responsible for the log and the production manager oversees all local production, including studio and remote broadcasts. The creative director works mainly with the production of commercial announcements and promotional spots. Some program departments will have a designated unit that is responsible for all local programming and spot announcements. This group keeps track of the materials, makes certain programs and spots are ready for air, which frequently means transferring them to a different medium, such as a computer hard drive. Sometimes this unit previews materials and performs a "gatekeeper" role, watching out for technically substandard materials or for content that needs to be reviewed. The same group handles shipping of programs being returned to syndicators.

Promotion

Broadcasters and cablecasters are constantly trying to attract an audience to their programming. Promotion on air and advertising in other media are necessities in mass media. Some news departments hire specialized promotion experts who prepare topical promotions based on current news, as well as more general spots. The promotion department generates TV listings, press releases, promotional brochures and other materials.

News

The majority of U.S. TV stations treat news as a separate department because news is frequently the station's major source of local programming and generates significant local revenue. At one time, news directors might answer to a program director, but over time, news departments have become so large and such a significant segment of local operations that most news directors have the same department head status as the program manager or the engineering manager. In recent times some stations have downgraded the role of program managers and upgraded news directors to a combined title, such as station manager and news director.

Engineering

The engineering department is responsible for the complex electronic plant of the television station. Engineering supervises the technicians who run the controls to put programming on the air, the technicians who run specialized equipment. Technicians program automated tape playback machines, program computers that carry out automatic tasks, monitor the quality of the picture and sound, repair and reprogram equipment, operate remote units, and maintain and operate satellite earth stations and the station's transmission equipment.

The senior engineering executive may be known internally as the chief engineer or director of engineering. The head of engineering supervises a team that has to comply with strict government technical rules. The concerns of the head of engineering range from personnel scheduling to long-term planning for major capital spending for new equipment and facilities.

Generally the engineering department will have several internal units, including personnel who run master control (through which all signals pass on the way to the transmitter); personnel who run other equipment; a maintenance unit; transmitter engineers; and operating technicians who may operate satellite trucks or earth stations. Depending on union agreements, the engineering department may provide technicians to run studio cameras; do studio lighting; install microphones; and run the audio control, video control, and switching operations in studio control rooms.

The engineering department in most broadcast facilities oversees several linked automation systems. Some of these include the following.

Automated Monitoring of Signal Quality and Transmission Equipment. The FCC sets has strict rules relating to the quality of the station's signal, and requires proof that the relevant functions are being monitored, either by people, or by proven reliable metering devices.

Automated Play-Out of Programs and Spots. The program log provides the database, but a separate system triggers all of the equipment that plays outs and routes and switches audio/video signals. One example of this type of automation is the *station break*, which occurs between two network programs. This used to be known as the *panic period* when live operators had to punch buttons and move levers in order to play out short commercial announcements and other spots and project slides while inserting audio. Sometimes they also had to load tapes. Today, the maximum level of human intervention frequently amounts to punching one button to start an automated sequence of events when the network transmits it trademark, which is the signal for stations to switch to the local commercial break.

A great deal of preparation goes into automated playout. The log data that triggers switching and playout has to be downloaded and checked for problems or errors. All the necessary materials have to be prepared, they frequently have to have a super-market type "bar code" printed and attached, and the timing and production details must be correct. Every spot and locally originated program is checked and loaded into a playback device, either an automated videotape playback unit, or a digital disk player. The log data that triggers switching and playout has to be downloaded and checked for problems or errors.

The greater part of production equipment is automated. We have spoken of character generators, still stores, Chromakeys, prompters, studio cameras, lighting, and virtual studios. When these devices run properly, they eliminate labor and errors. When they break down, manual control and a quick fix are in order.

Software and hardware maintenance is ongoing. Engineering departments follow preventive maintenance schedules, hoping to eliminate or reduce equipment malfunctions. When equipment fails to run, or computers don't function properly, they have to be fixed. Some equipment and computer hardware needs frequent adjustment. In the case of computers, this can be as simple, yet as important, as clearing unneeded data off hard disks.

Management Information Systems

More and more broadcast and cable facilities have a special department that has responsibility for computers and computer systems. Management Information Systems departments, often called the MIS department, may be freestanding or part of another unit. They advise on hardware and software purchases, monitor and maintain large computers, write computer programs, and in many cases, provide trainers, installers, and repair technicians for the organization.

With the increasing need for linking several distinct computer systems within organizations, there is a need for overall supervision of the systems, as well as the writing of specific programs to accomplish this integration of systems.

There is a rapid transition occurring in the broadcast and cable industries that finds people with MIS or computer training, taking over the engineering functions that were previously performed by people with electronics or electrical engineering backgrounds.

Master Control

The master control area in any large television facility is usually jammed with steel shelving or racks full of electronic devices with colored lights blinking on their faces. In midroom, one or two technicians will usually be found sitting in swivel chairs facing banks of colored buttons, levers, computer keyboards, and telephones.

The mystery to the casual observer is that the actions of the technicians frequently do not appear to be related to the rapidly changing images on the TV monitor screens. Master control technicians usually don't have to intervene with current programming, so they are frequently busy setting up sequences that will take place later. One important duty is to constantly check the quality of all output and quickly spot and remedy malfunctions.

Multiple station owners are increasingly centralizing the monitoring and operation of the transmitters and master control facilities of several stations into one control center at one of their facilities. The operators you see when you tour one of these stations may be monitoring the automation systems and transmitters of several stations, as well as managing their intake and distribution of programming via satellites, fiber optic circuits, or the Internet.

Another answer to the mystery of what do the technicians do relates to training and experience. The type of person who functions successfully in a master control setting is able to be calm even though there appears to be a lot going on, and indeed, there may be a lot of functions being executed. Modern automation systems have significantly reduced the need for having humans around to intervene. One example of this type of automation is the Weather Channel, which is so automated that one technician may be supervising the on air programming and monitoring several transmission feeds at the same time. One gets a similar impression walking through the transmission control areas of CNN.

What kinds of automated activities are taking place in master control?

One or more streams of programming are passing through routing switchers, on their way to microwave links, uplinks, fiber optic cables, or transmitters and towers, which is known as *program transmission*. Switching from network to a local break to the local news broadcast is highly automated, requiring either no human action or at the least, one "commit" action, which involves pushing a button.

Monitoring for quality is being done by electronic metering devices. Technicians check readouts regularly and are ready to respond if warning devices go off. Activity will pick up if there is a loss of signal or electrical power. A technician may have to manually control a sequence to return a transmitter to the air or power up a generator if its automatic starter fails. They are usually responsible for monitoring tower lighting and performance as well.

Most of the frantic activity related to switching among incoming or outgoing sources has been taken over by computers. Usually a dedicated system switches on recording devices and realigns satellite dishes to focus on satellites and transponders for the dozens of satellite feeds that arrive daily. Most of the technical work in the satellite area concentrates on feeding the right data into the computer.

Automated Production (Studio Control)

In order for a local television program to be produced in a studio, there must be a control room to house much of the electronic equipment and provide means to switch and combine various inputs.

COMPUTERS IN THE CONTROL ROOM

Video. A news broadcast may require three or more studio cameras. Added to this can be remotely controlled cameras installed in the newsroom and news bureaus. Many stations have remote-controlled cameras installed in various places in their coverage area to provide weather and traffic pictures. Other external sources include microwave vans and satellite trucks and sources of prepared video, which include tape playback units, automated tape playback machines, or digital disk players.

Camera automation is a well-developed science. Broadcasters moved to automated cameras for news broadcasts because studio cameras do not get used to their highest potential during a news broadcast. Most shots in news programs are static, that is, head and shoulder or medium shots of the anchors. There is little zooming in or out, or complex "trucks" or "dollies" in which the camera moves while the shot is on the air. Therefore using three or four camera operators becomes an added financial burden. Some small stations solved the personnel problem by using three or four live cameras on the news set, but hiring only two part-time college students, who moved from camera to camera, setting up the shots.

In markets where it wasn't feasible or practical to use part-time employees in this manner, stations and networks began to look at camera automation. Cameras could be controlled from the technical director's position in the studio control room. Some broadcasters prefer to station one camera operator at a control console in the studio. The operator can react quicker and pay closer attention to the camera shots. In point of fact, the on-air camera has a camera operator, but the person is not

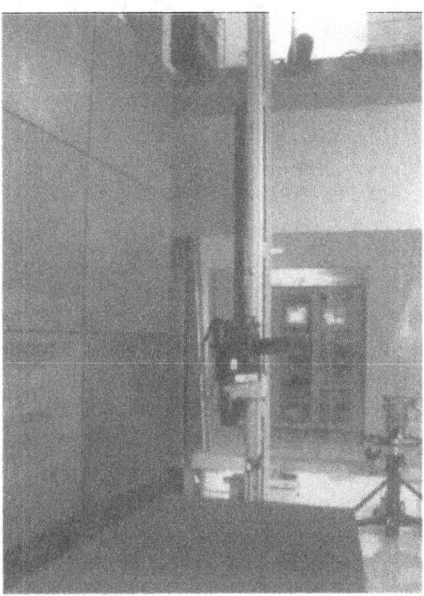

FIG. 7.1. A wall-mounted robotic camera trolley system. This system can be mounted vertically or horizontally. The camera mounting is servo controlled allowing for very precise movements. Photo courtesy of Telemetrics Incorporated.

standing behind the camera. Instead, the operator controls the camera from a console and, therefore, is able to set up shots on the remaining cameras. This technique has resulted in significant savings in technician wages for some broadcasters.

There are several technologies available to assure that a camera moves to its designated spot on the floor. Some of the control systems were adapted from military gunnery technology. Some run on tracks on the floor.

It is possible to program camera shots into the rundown using a newsroom computer, but this is not yet a common feature of automation. What is becoming increasingly common is the installation of all-weather, remote-controllable cameras at key locations around a community. The technology is similar to observation cameras installed in town centers and other public locations by police in Britain and the United States. These cameras can be manipulated by remote control. They started out mainly as a way to observe weather conditions or traffic congestion but soon proved their worth when particularly visual news events occurred.

One dramatic example occurred when Miami television station WTVJ-TV focused one of its 13 remote-site cameras on smoke billowing out of a cruise ship and then secured a voice description of what was happening from an eyewitness aboard the ship who spoke to the TV station on a cellular telephone.

Graphics. The character generator, the DVE (digital video effects) device, the still store, and the Chromakey can all be programmed by the newsroom computer system. The weather graphics computer could be integrated into the newsroom system, but is usually a separate installation programmed by the weatherperson.

Alphanumeric. The prompter and the closed-captioning unit were some of the first devices linked to the newsroom computer system.

Lights. Lights may be remotely controlled by commands embedded in the news script.

Audio. Studios have an audio mixing board to switch and control studio mikes and all sound sources. In simple installations a technique called *audio-follow-video* can be set up in which the audio is switched automatically by video switch. For more complex newscasts, many stations prefer to have an audio operator. There is also an intercommunication system so that control room personnel can talk with studio production personnel and the talent, as well as staff members at live remotes.

A first visit to a large station or network studio control room is frequently confusing. During election coverage, there may be 30 or more people seated in a network control room. They are performing very specific functions that are part of a complex production.

Despite the number of people present, the level of noise created by people speaking is minimal. It's typical to anticipate shouting and frenetic activity as you tiptoe into a network control room. You are more likely to find a director sitting at a desk

FIG. 7.2. The device mounted on the front of the Sony camera is a "prompter." The script is fed from the newsroom computer system to the horizontal screen at the left. The screen image is reflected on the one-way mirror mounted diagonally in front of the camera lens. The anchorperson reads the projected script from the surface of the mirror, while the camera lens is feeding the anchor's image to the control room. Image courtesy of Computer Prompting & Captioning Co.

next to the technical director (where all the lighted buttons are located) calmly holding up a yellow pencil, and as the pencil dips, saying softly but firmly "take four." Again, professionalism requires a "calm in the middle of a storm" demeanor from the person at the center of the production activity.

A great deal of the actual talking is going on over the headset circuit, where people speak softly and only when they need to speak to give directions or ask questions. The director and the technical director may be hearing a lot more in their phones than is indicated by their actions. "Cleveland is ready on R-13 ... camera two loosen up ... tapes, do you have Beirut yet? ... tell the White House they get 2 minutes. ... Beirut ready ... roll VTR 9 ... take V9.... Tell Cleveland they're next.... Disk malfunction on 20, use 22 instead ... coming out ... ready talent, ready one, cue talent and take." Somewhere back of the director a producer speaks into another circuit: "Cleveland, standby ... we're dropping the Q&A for time, give us one sentence on camera and a lock-out ... stand by ... in ten ... five, four, three, two, and ... go."

The more complex the production, the more difficult it is to automate. A local station broadcast on a quiet day could be run directly from the producer's rundown

FIG. 7.3. This is what an anchorperson sees when facing the prompter-equipped camera. Image courtesy of Computer Prompting & Captioning Co.

if all the necessary equipment were tied into the automation system. An entry on the rundown or a script functions as an instruction to a device. There is still a preference for having a director or producer make the actual decision to commit something to air, to preserve timing and control. The automated tape or disk playback unit can be programmed to have each tape or file ready, the CG can be preprogrammed, as can the still store and other devices.

There is another solution using automation. It consists of prerecording, "packaging," each element of a broadcast. Instead of inserting a CG while a videotape is playing, the CG is recorded as part of a packaged story. The latest digital technology goes a long way to make it possible to prepackage stories in editing rooms.

Each finished segment is transferred over a computer network to a digital disk server. Anchor appearances can be either live or prerecorded. If all the elements are stored on a digital disk, the broadcast can be run directly from a newsroom computer located in the control room. This works for one 30-minute news broadcast, or several hours. This "mix-and-match" technique of producing the news, which combines prerecorded anchor appearances and taped stories or features, is used by CNN and several local all-news cable channels. It is possible to run a news program with one person controlling the automation system.

A computer system in the newsroom proves its value during a news broadcast when a decision is made to change the order of news stories. Most systems have features that allow a producer to move stories with a few clicks of the computer mouse. The system automatically changes the order and recalculates the time. It also changes the order of the copy in the prompting system. Although it is appropriate to advise the anchors of the change, copy shuffling is not a critical issue as long as the anchors are skilled at reading off a prompter screen. This sort of change was a nightmare when anchors relied on paper scripts and prompting systems that required papers scripts.

The combining of newsroom computer systems and machine control has affected employment levels in production departments, but perhaps not as much as one would think. The major savings are in eliminating certain high-pressure situations that were prone to mistakes. The combination of computer-based rundowns and automatic playback equipment has led to fewer tape loading errors. It also cuts down on the number of personnel needed to look after the tape playback units.

Some organizations had operators running the prompting systems. Computer technology has eliminated the need for most prompter operators. Less time and effort has to be expended on graphics because slide files have been replaced by computer memory within still store devices. Graphic artists use computers to speed up production of visuals for the news department. These graphics can be downloaded into the still store for automatic playout.

Character generators still need some human intervention because most broadcasts call for new names not in the computer's memory. Generally running the CG is now a part time activity for a bright production assistant.

Overall, these automated production devices have cut back on hiring of some studio production workers and technicians. Within television stations, this technology transition has also shifted the internal power structure. In many cases the production director has fewer people to supervise. News directors, with added staff and more direct involvement in production, have moved up in corporate hierarchies.

Even with all the advances in newsroom computer technology and improvements in the automation of production devices, most news programs are put on the air from a director's desk. In smaller stations, the director not only controls the order and production values of the broadcast, he or she actually punches buttons, moves levers and rotates "joy sticks" to make events happen within the broadcast. In large organizations, or where union jurisdiction rules apply, a technical director sits next to the director. The technical director carries out all of the actual switching, fading, starting, and stopping associated with directing a broadcast.

A NEW WAY TO DIRECT A NEWS BROADCAST

In recent years, new automation technology has been introduced to allow one person to direct a broadcast, using a computer keyboard and software that "builds" an event timeline before a broadcast begins. At this writing, one company, ParkerVision, Inc. (PVTV) is the major vendor of this technology. PVTV introduced its technology to broadcasters when it won the contract to equip the control room for a cable news channel serving the Borough of the Bronx in New York City. The news channel could staff its newsroom with a production assistant, a producer, and a director. Company representatives have said that if the director were ill and couldn't come to work, the producer could direct the news blocks and still do the tasks a producer regularly performs.

PVTV is a computer program that relies on coding each event that occurs during a broadcast. In a conventional TV station newsroom, the creator of a story must insert these codes in the script at the point where an event occurs. In other words, you would have to code for the on-camera anchor, the roll for the VO (video over voice), the insert point for a SOT (sound on tape) insert, the VO video out, and the return to the anchorperson. This information is transferred to the director's computer where the software automatically starts, integrates, and stops each event.

The director spends considerable time prior to the broadcast setting up what are called *timelines* that preprogram all the events in the broadcast. There is very little switching done during the broadcast, although some directors prefer to insert character generator images live in order to assure insertion at the proper point. The system has override keys to permit live switches for breaking news, and the software includes dozens of typical switching sequences that can be selected during programming. If the need arises, the director can intervene and go to manual control.

One installation we visited had studio cameras mounted on robotic heads. Once the camera pedestal was positioned, the director controlled its tilt, swivel, and lens focus functions from the control room. If the camera needed to be trucked or dollied to a new position, the floor manager repositioned the camera. Robotic cameras can be mounted on tracks that go up and down a wall or post, or on rods hanging from the ceiling. Typically, this type of automation reduces the floor crew from two or more camera operators and a floor manager to just a floor manager.

It does take some time to set up the computer time-lines, so a director may end up spending more time working on the news broadcasts, and less time doing production. One station found that it had to plan for coding time by an assistant director and the director in order to handle multiple news broadcasts airing back-to-back.

Staff reaction to this newest form of automation was predictably reserved. The reporters, anchors, and producers all had to learn the coding procedure. The major fault with this approach is that a coding mistake that is not caught can disrupt a broadcast. The least happy staff members we interviewed were meteorologists, who have a great deal of computer work to do just getting their forecasts ready, and they found the coding a major challenge, especially considering the number of switching events that take place during a weather segment.

There is every indication that the use of this latest form of production automation will spread rapidly, and may become the *de facto* standard for directing news broadcasts.

FIG. 7.4. A director running a news broadcast from a ParkerVision computer keyboard. Picture courtesy of WCTV, Tallahassee, Florida.

ANOTHER ENGINEERING FUNCTION: AIRING SPOT ANNOUNCEMENTS

Keeping track of and playing spot announcements is a complex activity for commercial television organizations. There are three kinds of announcements which must be considered: commercials, promotions, and public service announcements.

Once an advertiser orders a commercial schedule, arrangements are made to supply the commercial itself. It may arrive from a New York or Chicago ad agency (or its production house), a regional agency, a local agency, or it may be created in the station's studios. So the first step is get the actual commercial into the building. The next step is to make certain it is transferred to the proper medium for playout. There is a lack of standardization in tape playout technology among television broadcasters, so spots frequently have to be copied (i.e., dubbed) to the medium used by the broadcaster or cablecaster. Locally produced spots have a tendency to arrive late, which puts a great deal of pressure on station personnel.

A commercial announcement must also be reviewed for content and time. There are certain types of commercial claims which violate FCC or Federal Trade Commission regulations. Advertisers are unlikely to send an offending spot, but the broadcaster has the responsibility of checking anyway.

Time is important because time is money. If you pay for 30 seconds, that's what you get, not 35 seconds. The timing situation is further complicated because computers frequently do the switching from one item to another, and a computer that has been programmed to switch exactly at 30 seconds elapsed, will do as it was instructed whether there is still content on the tape or not.

Most broadcast facilities have an inventory of public service announcements that are currently scheduled to be run. Someone is designated to plan these campaigns and keep track of the spots run, and have them replaced at the end of their planned use. What is run is not random, it is planned, and records are kept in order to supply reports to community groups and the Federal Communications Commission.

Promotional announcements are essential to competitive video media. These consist of promotional announcements prepared to encourage viewing of network and syndicated programs, as well a locally prepared promotional announcements to highlight local programming.

Once the commercial announcements are in-house and checked for content and time (as well as compared with other records to make certain the right spots were shipped) they have to be prepared for use on the air. One method is to copy the spot to a tape cartridge that is used in an automated tape playback system. This requires the printing of a bar-code label. Some stations store spot announcements on digital playback devices. That means each spot has to be coded so it can be retrieved.

Promotional spots for news programs frequently require capturing excerpts or clips from current news stories and quickly producing a promo. Many promotion specialists do their own editing, which means knowing how to use one of the popular nonlinear editing systems.

The program traffic department enters all spot announcements into a file for the upcoming log. The commercials go where the sales department has placed them.

Then promotional announcements are inserted, with close attention being paid to not promoting a program that just concluded, or a program that is no longer shown on the station. Finally, public service spots are inserted.

The log, which appears in paper form and as a series of computer screens is then put into the traffic system, and in many facilities, automatically transferred to the production computer system that controls the devices that are going to play the spots. Automation has gotten to a state that it should be possible to log and load all of a station's spot commitments for a day during one work session, and anticipate they will play out when they are supposed to.

News producers do not have direct involvement with commercials, except to be aware of how much commercial time has been allotted around and within the broadcast. Time for breaks to run the commercials has to be deducted from overall program time. Astute producers check on the specific commercials, promos, or public service announcements that are scheduled within their program in order to avoid embarrassing adjacencies between the news content and the commercials. Sometimes a producer will move a story away from a spot if the change does not interfere with the news presentation. Maybe the Last National Bank was robbed this afternoon, and it has a spot scheduled next to the local news section. The bank's agency may want to move the spot or take a replacement later (called a *make-good*).

Occasionally a producer will flag management to a possible conflict between news content and a commercial. Say, for instance, Harry's Pizza Parlor has a spot scheduled during the news. Unfortunately, Harry was arrested earlier today by the authorities for not paying the government the social security portion of his employees' wages. A sharp producer should let the news director and the sales department know about the adjacency. The news story won't be dropped, but sales might want to make a phone call and see if Harry's spots should be moved or canceled.

For a long time the airline industry requested that all airline spots be dropped whenever a commercial passenger aircraft crashed. In this case, an immediate call to sales and business is very much appreciated.

CONCLUSION

If you were to look for jobs dealing with automation in a television facility, the place to start would be in engineering, where the subsystems in the news department and the traffic department merge into the computer that actually runs the facility. It may also communicate with other computers that receive satellite feeds or switch the destinations of program and satellite feeds. It is wise to learn how these systems relate to each other, not to become a computer expert but simply to know how programming gets on the air. It is much easier to solve a production problem when the parties understand the system and each other. Producers have to constantly solve production problems with the help of engineering and computer experts.

8

Computer-Assisted Reporting

The melding of the PC and the Internet has given journalists a vast warehouse of information, as well as an inexpensive means of communication.

The Internet was created by the U.S. Department of Defense during the 1960s to provide a communication medium for scientists working on defense projects. Gradually it expanded to 50 sites, many on university campuses. In the early 1980s the network (called ARPANET) was opened to users who did not have security clearances and its name was changed to the Internet.

The Internet is a decentralized, megastorehouse composed of millions of hosts, called *domain* computers, each with thousands of users. The Internet was somewhat of a "cult" communication medium for the computer-literate until early in the 1990s when the public became aware of its capabilities.

The World Wide Web (WWW) in web addresses was the creation of Tim Berners-Lee, an Oxford University trained physicist who maintains an office at the Massachusetts Institute of Technology in Cambridge. In 1980, while a consultant at CERN, an European physics laboratory, Berners-Lee wrote a program named *Enquire*. The program allowed Berners-Lee to mark words in a document so that when a user "clicked" on these words, the user would be led to other documents that provided additional information. This process is called *hypertext*. In 1989 Berners-Lee returned to the CERN lab, and secured financing to set up a computer as the first Web server.

Berners-Lee is credited with writing the first software for servers. He and his colleagues also developed three important elements of Web technology. They were the language used to encode documents, HTML (hypertext markup language); the system used to link documents, HTTP (hypertext transfer protocol); and the *www.*_____ system of addresses, called a URL (universal resource locator).[1]

---

[1]Wright, R. (1997). *The man who invented the Web.* Time, Inc.: New York. Reprinted in: Wickham, K. Ed. (1998), *Perspectives: Online journalism.* Boulder, Colorado: CourseWise Publishing. pp. 5–9.

The business community, sensing new opportunities, leapt at the opportunity, and began turning out software to make Internet communication easier for an average computer user. No one knows how many Internet users there are, but the Internet now circles the globe and continues to grow exponentially.[2]

The conversion of broadcast newsroom computer systems to PC-based systems at about the same time opened up information resources that had never before been conveniently available for broadcast journalists. For instance, many newspapers maintained libraries or *morgues*. Typically these contained copies of previous editions, clippings files on a wide variety of topics, and standard reference books. In most cases, the in-house resources available to newspaper journalists far exceeded the research files of a broadcast newsroom, which were more likely to consist solely of tapes and scripts of earlier broadcasts.

The Internet doesn't discriminate. The smallest news organization can have the same resources as a major market broadcaster. The computer terminal on our desk helps us by opening doors to information. In this chapter, we go through those doors and see where cyberspace leads us.

WHAT IS FILED IN THE SYSTEM ARCHIVES?

Most broadcast newsroom computer systems in use today include an archives function. It provides producers, the assignment desk, reporters, and writers with a convenient way to store and access scripts and rundowns from prior broadcasts. It should index videotaped copies of the broadcasts or individual stories in the broadcast so that the tapes can be reviewed, or excerpts taken out to illustrate current news stories. An archives system can index digital copies of stories that are retained in computer servers.

The customary way to handle archiving is to delegate someone to file the day's scripts and rundowns to a special archives program. The reason a special program is necessary is that the archives have to hold a lot of data, so that part of the newsroom system needs to have a lot of memory. Archives programs have specialized software to assist your in searching for data. The software compresses the data so more can be stored.

The latest trend is to create what one company calls a *digital asset management/archives system*. This type of system is used at CNN, which has about 20 years worth of news video. CNN's *Headline News* alone is estimated to carry 7,000 pieces of video each week.[3]

If you are fortunate, you might remember the day and even time that a certain story ran. More likely, you simply need to gather some background information very quickly. Say a long-serving member of the city council has a serious heart at-

---

[2]Based on: Wendland, M. (1996). *Wired Journalist: newsroom guide to the Internet.* Radio and Television News Directors Foundation: Washington DC. pp. 5–6.

[3]Grotticelli, M. (May, 1998). *Sony to provide CNN with ENG equipment.* Television/Broadcast: New York. pp. 9, 36.

tack and dies. You have to get together an obituary. Unlike the big network news organizations, most smaller news organizations do not have enough staff to prepare obituaries ahead of time. The archives program comes to the rescue. You bring up the archives file and ask it to search, using the council member's name, for stories from which you can extract biographical information. The technique for searching varies from program to program, but in general you enter the information you have in descending order, such as town or city, title, last name, first name.

Searching for information on your local council member should be easy. What you do not want to do is start a search with no more than a common name. Imagine what would happen if you were asked to prepare a backgrounder on former President Bill Clinton, and so all you entered was CLINTON. You would get every Clinton who was ever mentioned in your files, plus Clinton, Iowa; Clinton Street, and who knows what else. The moment you narrow your search to Clinton, Bill, President, the search becomes a little more focused. Because presidents are in the news a great deal, you would probably want to keep narrowing your search. You could add, *taxation*, to get stories about tax legislation, for example.

Most archives programs tell you how many items they have retrieved before you have to actually sort through the items. If the count comes up 10,013, you know you have to refine the search!

Most newsroom archives programs are designed to store scripts and related data. Some may permit you to add other items, such as individual wire stories, or a set of notes. Technology is available that will permit these systems to hold low-resolution versions of news tape. It can be previewed at a workstation, rather than having to be withdrawn from the tape file room, and played on a VTR. Many newsroom computer systems are capable of holding several days worth of wire service input, so a short-range search may be possible by going to the wire file. All wire files eventually purge copy, usually on the basis that it is so many hours or days old. If the system didn't clean out the old copy, the computers would run out of storage capability, and the whole system might "freeze." However, it may be possible to go to the wire service archives, giving you a new research dimension.

USING THE INTERNET

Internet connectivity is almost universal in today's broadcast newsrooms. Access, however, is sometimes restricted to avoid having unauthorized people tying up the system, or in some cases, creating a huge provider service bill. The basic requirements for Internet access are having a computer with a modem to process your signal attached to a telephone or dedicated data line. Internet users, unless they are very large organizations, usually subscribe to one of dozens of available services. The service provides a local telephone number or data line and the computer technology to connect the user to the Internet. The modem is a device that acts like a telephone for the computer. Telephone companies and cable companies also offer special high-speed premium services in some areas.

Let's look at two of the major features of the Internet:

COMPUTER-BASED REPORTING   133

Electronic Mail

Electronic mail, known as e-mail, is one of the great features of the Internet. You can send and receive messages around the world. Some people actually answer their e-mail before they deal with telephone calls. Some reporters use e-mail to set appointments and gather background information for their stories. E-mail is also useful for receiving documents and news releases.

When you go to work for a news organization, the person in charge of the computer system will probably issue you a password, which allows you to use the system. In addition, you may be given a specific e-mail address, such as: smithg@ZZZZ.com. The *g* would stand for your first name because Smith is a common name. The four Zs would be the station's call letters. The news department might have a general address, such as: newsctr8@zzzz.com.

Electronic Mailing Lists. Thousands of interest groups have set up mailing lists, sometimes known as *listservs*. The list is installed in a central computer that receives all incoming mail and then automatically sends the message to all the subscribers. Each list has a procedure for subscribing, so you have to get a copy of subscription information from someone, and then follow the simple instructions. If the newsroom or library has a copy of Mike Wendland's *Wired Journalist: Newsroom Guide to the Internet,* published by the Radio and Television News Directors Foundation, several of these lists are described in Appendix D.

Practically every broadcast journalist with access to e-mail subscribes to the free newsletter *ShopTalk*, which is circulated by Don Fitzpatrick, a veteran industry talent recruiter (for information go to www.tvspy.com). It contains the latest trade rumors, and instructions how to access a job list. Regular readers of *ShopTalk* recognize news stories that show up on television a day or two after a discussion item appeared in *ShopTalk*. Some lists send material daily, others ebb and flow as members decide to enter messages.

A variation on the mailing list are newsgroups. Subscribers post discussion topics and comments. These are good sources of ideas for stories.

The government has mailing lists. For example, the Federal Communications Commission puts out a summary of its activities on weekdays. The summary includes both World Wide Web and telephone contacts for further information. A private foundation puts out media headlines daily. Brief summaries follow the headlines, which are taken from media publications and media-knowledgeable newspapers.

There are a number of other features that become useful to information gathering as you gain experience with e-mail and the Internet.

Other E-Mail. You can e-mail articles or scripts. These can be typed within the e-mail word-processor, or if you prefer a more sophisticated approach, you can prepare an article or script using your regular word-processor, and then copy it and move to the e-mail message function, where you can paste it in the message section of the screen. You may also specify it as an attachment and simply list the file name. Audio, still photos, and video can also be transferred by e-mail. Ryan Gerding, a reporter for KCRG-TV in Cedar Rapids, Iowa, found a clever way to illustrate a local story:

> The first time I used the Internet to make a significant, tangible impact on a television story was in my coverage of the arrest of a suspected bank robber in Iowa. Dubuque, Iowa police officers had arrested and charged a man with robbing a bank in town. Police told me the man confessed to robbing the bank in Dubuque and several others in North Carolina. I called the photo desks at two North Carolina newspapers where the robberies happened. When their papers covered their own bank robberies, they ran still photos of the security camera videos. I had a still picture from the robbery in Iowa. Both photo editors agreed to trade pictures with me over the Internet. I e-mailed them my picture, and they e-mailed me theirs. It took all of about 30 minutes to do the entire exchange. So, while the other stations showed boring maps in their stories to show where the other robberies happened, I showed security camera pictures from the actual robberies. (personal communication, August 3, 1998)

E-mail can be used to send story files and even video from the field when an organization has the proper equipment. E-mail can also bring in information. Many stations and reporters put e-mail addresses on the screen, letterheads, and business cards and end up getting news tips via the Internet.

The World Wide Web

The World Wide Web (WWW) consists of "pages" that you can reach through the Internet. The pages are interactive. They can display text and pictures, and some can supply audio and video. Many World Wide Web pages are interactive in the sense that you can move the computer cursor to a highlighted word or phrase on the screen, and when you click the mouse, you will connect to another page with further information (hypertext).

Let's say your school has a Web site (and most do). Once you reach the first or cover page, you would be given the opportunity to click on several options. These might include the school calendar, admissions, scholarships, schools and colleges, sports, activities, a list of faculty, and a directory of administrative offices.

Anyone can create a Web page. Generally though, it takes quite a lot of skill to create a good Web page or site, which is identified by its *URL,* or *Universal Resource Locator,* which is its address. A URL address always begins with: http:// followed by www and the rest of the address. If you wanted to access the ShopTalk homepage (another name for a Web page or Web site) to learn more about jobs in broadcast journalism, you would select the location function of your Internet software, and then type in: http://www.tvspy.com. Some locators know you mean http:// when you type in www, so you don't have to type the clumsy http:// prefix.

What Does WWW Do for You?

The opening screen of most Internet software provides ways to search for information you need but don't know where to find. A search begins at the *search engine,* which is a specific software program that goes looking for information on the Internet. Next you enter either key words or a short description of what you are trying to find. Search engines generally provide on-screen guidance on how to write your search inquiry.

In a matter of seconds you will get a report on how many *hits* or items the search engine has found as well as a list, with the items that most closely march your search at the top. You can read the list, click on an item of interest and look at it, and if it seems useful, print out the file. Then point your cursor to one of the *return* or *back* functions, and you will return to the list, which you can scroll through looking for items of interest.

Search engines vary, but any computer search works better if you carefully think out the information you are seeking, and use the tips on searching to construct a logical inquiry. Generally, construct your search so that you narrow large categories as much as possible.

There are search shortcuts that save a great deal of time. These are constantly changing and are best learned from the various guides put out by journalists' groups, such as Radio and Television News Directors Foundation (RTNDF) and the Society of Professional Journalists. After you have learned how to do searches, you will start picking up hints on time saving methods from other Internet users.

Finding two or three good sites is exciting, but it is only one step in the reporting process. Most of the information you gather will open doors for you, but it may not be unbiased, definitive, or correct. It is raw information.

If you are wondering about the authenticity of a site, you can go to a domain registration site to check on who owns the site. The registration site will ask you to type in the URL you are checking.

Typical Sites in Your Coverage Area

The Web is so universal that you should have site addresses for most of the people and places you have listed in your personal telephone diary. Local governments have sites. Many municipalities and counties have given up sending out paper agendas for upcoming meetings, preferring to refer people to their Web site, which the Internet user can access and print out the agenda, at very little cost to the city or country.

Local and state government departments have both informational and data sites. The latter are sites that permit you to retrieve information that is public record. Once you find these locations, you can save a lot of time, compared to having to go to a government building to inspect files. One example is county property records. Many real estate firms use the Internet to retrieve ownership data. Reporters can access these files, too. One typical use would be to investigate whether or not a local politician had his or her primary residence in the district she or he represents. (This assumes residence in one's district is a requirement of state law.) Counties or states keep vital statistics, such as birth and death records, which can be helpful to investigative reporters.

Chambers of commerce, travel and convention bureaus, associations, colleges, and universities frequently have Web sites. You can find lists of experts by checking databases of experts. One such site is www.Profnet1.com.

You will find Web sites listed on TV programs, in the telephone book, and in ads. Save the ones that you think might be useful. If you use a site and you think you might want to return to it, move your cursor to the *Bookmark* function and store the address. The next time you want to visit the site, open up Bookmark and scroll to the site address. It's a big time-saver.

Freelance journalist/producer Shannon Reichley (personal communication, August 6, 1998) recalls how using the Internet broke an interesting local story in sports-conscious Charlotte, North Carolina:

> In 1996, Charlotte's new NFL stadium was built and just months away from being in use, but had not been officially named, as word was that $20 million could buy your name on it. One morning, a friend of one of one of our staffers (who was in advertising) called to say he'd seen a sketch for a logo that said *ericson* on the stadium, and that a press conference might be in the wind. Since all assumed that a local company would be the logo sponsor, we started to the cast the net, but got no comments from the Stadium Authority. For fun, I got on the Internet and searched for *ericson*. That didn't surface, but *Ericcson* did, and I went to that company's Web site (they're based in Sweden ... fiber optics and cellphones).
>
> Long story short, they had an operation in N.C., I called PR there, she sounded confused, but confirmed the stadium deal. We went with the story at 6 (the NFL didn't deny it), and they had the press conference the next day. Without the Web, we would not have had the resources to figure out so quickly what Ericcson was, and what the connection was.

Todd Halliday, News Director of WDEL-AM in Wilmington, Delaware searches area newspapers via a site called www.NewsIndex.com. It points him to newspaper articles about Delaware, and provides ideas for unique local stories. The same strategy would be very effective for a small-market television station.

Marsha Redmon, consumer law reporter for WCNC-TV in Charlotte, North Carolina used the Internet to gather information about an accident on a holiday, when virtually none of the station's primary sources were available by telephone.

> We had a helicopter crash in the early morning hours of Memorial Day this year. When I arrived to work the holiday, I used the Internet to do a story about the safety record of that specific aircraft, the company that flew it, and the history of helicopter crashes in North and South Carolina. All on the Internet. I could not get anyone on the phone since it was a holiday. Fortunately, I knew about a few sites that collect

crash and accident data because I attended a NICAR (National Institute of Computer Assisted Reporting) "boot camp" at the University of Missouri. A great course. (personal communication, August 4, 1998)

Chris Heinbaugh at KOMO-TV in Seattle has used computer assisted reporting techniques at his current station and at KNXV-TV in Phoenix. He said:

One popular use is matching one database with another, looking for matches in common fields like first or last names, and birth date. In 1997, while at KNXV, we matched a state database of licensed EMTs (emergency medical technicians) and paramedics with a database we created of criminal court records. We ended up with more than a thousand matches, each case of which, had to be opened and reviewed to confirm identities, and then see the nature and the outcome of the case. With that as our foundation, our investigation went on to disclose rules to the contrary, dozens of convicted criminals were certified as EMTs and Paramedics by the state. We revealed that they slipped through the cracks by lying on their applications, and that the state didn't catch this because they weren't bothering to do background checks, relying on the honor system instead. One case we discovered was of a convicted thief who lied on his application, and went on to steal from patients. After he was caught and convicted, he went to another state and did the same thing. We found him in a third state where he had been certified after lying on his application.

Another way we use CAR (computer assisted reporting) is to run queries (ask questions) of the data contained in the databases. Asking the question several different ways can reveal all sorts of surprises, and just the facts you need.

In 1996, Circle K, a major corporation was trying to boost sales of its convenience store gas. So it joined forces with Unocal, and launched a huge ad campaign telling consumers that high-quality Unocal 76 was now in the pumps. But through some extensive, pavement-pounding journalism, we discovered that the gas at the pumps was the same stuff that was there before. Nothing had really changed.

But these were big companies, and big advertisers, and we were looking for more proof. We found it in an inspection database at the Arizona Department of Weights and Measures. By pulling out all the inspection records for Circle K, we could determine beyond any doubt that all the gas at those stations came from the old supplier, not Unocal's refinery. We also used it to debunk Circle K claims that everyone did it, because it showed that other stations got their gas from their own brand's refinery. And finally, the inspection data showed that, despite Circle K claims that the quality was the same, the level of quality violations was really much higher than Unocal's. Our report sparked an investigation by the Attorney General's office, which ended in a settlement with Circle K.

Heinbaugh said CAR can be used to share information with viewers:

At KOMO, we were doing a story on doctors who have been disciplined by the state. As part of our report, we compiled a list of all doctors who had been under some disciplinary sanction by state medical regulators at some point since 1990. We used this as an organizational tool for looking at several hundred cases. This was public information, but we also realized that few patients really knew how, or the importance of checking on their doctors' disciplinary past. So we took the information, and compiled a pamphlet listing more than 200 doctors, the charges, and the action taken against them. We offered it free to our viewers, and have received almost 35,000 requests. We also made it available on our Web site in a pdf file (graphics) download, and have had thousands of downloads. We continue to maintain and update it as a public service to our viewers, and nine months later, we still get about 50–100 requests for pamphlets each week. (personal communication, August 19, 1998)

Computer assisted reporting does not have to involve complicated database matches. Heinbaugh said:

I have accumulated and processed databases of criminal records, sex offender registries, drivers licenses, voter registration records that our staff uses each day to track down people. Also, in Washington state, our court system is online, allowing us access to basic information about these cases. Our State Patrol also provides on-line access to criminal background checks. These are tools that have evolved from "specialized" status, into everyday tools we turn to instinctively, and give us an edge over our competition.

Special Answers to Special Problems
Chris Heinbaugh, Reporter

MAKING C-A-R INVESTIGATIONS GOOD TV/Some suggestions:

1. Don't let the computer become the story.

It's okay to share the process with viewers. In fact, it lends credibility to your story. But remember, it is not the story. Sometimes, we get so enamored with the computer work we did, or want to let everyone know how much work it took, or want to impress colleagues ... that it plays a bigger role than it should. Keep the role to a minimum.

2. The data must support a story.

Findings by themselves mean nothing. They tend to impress journalists and insiders, but you still have to build your story, and find the elements to make viewers angry and care. Your discoveries using CAR are only the beginning. You can't just stop there. You must have a story.

3. Find real people.

This seems basic, yet it's the element that, in the rush to be first, is easy to leave behind. If your story really is important, then there has to be somebody or something impacted by what you've found. And avoid the "Man on the Street" angle. It's cheap and easy. This part of your story is just as important as the data, and even more so in selling it. Invest the time. It's worth it.

4. Know the strengths of your medium.

This is television, not print or radio. You need a good story, emotion, and video. Television is not worse or better than print for CAR stories, just different. Knowing what works and what doesn't can mean the difference between a story that moves viewers to action, and one that moves them to use the remote.

5. Keep your findings to the bare minimum.

During the course of your investigation, you may come up with many interesting and even pertinent information and trails. But trying to squeeze everything in, may weaken your best discoveries. Pick your strongest points, and build your story around those. If they're strong enough, they may deserve to be stories on their own, great follow-up material, or can be used peripherally, perhaps on your Web site.

6. Don't overload your story with facts and numbers.

It's always a difficult balance. You want enough to back up your investigation, but not too many to lose the viewer. And keep them simple. Viewers can't stop and ponder a complicated graph or multiple sets of numbers. If they do, they're probably missing the next few sentences of the track.

7. Use graphics to help tell your story.

If you need a graphic to emphasize a point, use it. But be careful ... uncreative, confusing graphics can stop a story in its tracks. And too many graphics could leave your viewer wondering about the point of the story.

8. Use your computer to help tell the story.

Creative shooting and good teamwork with your photographer can help you avoid graphics altogether. Remember, there is natural sound present when using the computer. Keyboard, a mouse, CD-ROM, beeps, etc. And elements of the computer can highlight elements in your story. Cursors, arrows, highlight keys, etc. Creative use of these can help you avoid graphics, and still make the points hit home.

[reproduced with the permission of Chris Heinbaugh]

FIG. 8.1. This elaborate news set was designed and built for KRON television in San Francisco by FX GroupFXScenery and Display. It features a rear projection screen with a digital projector. The anchor platform/desk is on casters so that it can be rotated to permit the rear projection screen to be used as a stand-up position. The second floor of the set has a 12-inch electronic ticker in the face of the balcony. There are approximately 80 monitors on the set, which also has robotic cameras. This set was moved from Orlando, Florida, to San Francisco in a 53-foot trailer. An eight-person crew took five days to erect the set and install the lighting. Image courtesy of FX Group/FX Scenery and Display, Ocoee, Florida.

THE FEDERAL GOVERNMENT

The Internet has been a big help to people needing information from the federal government. Government departments now post the information most consumers seek. These agencies also post news releases, policy statements, speech transcripts, and official decisions or policies. The U.S. Census is a useful source of statistics.

Various regulatory agencies keep track of businesses and other organizations by requiring periodic filing of financial records and other reports. Once you learn how to read these reports, you can uncover a great deal of information about a business or organization.

Political parties and thousands of groups and individuals having concerns about government operations also maintain sites. Many members of Congress have Web sites.

Some of the most interesting information about federal concerns comes from organizations that lobby for special interests, or maintain a "watchdog" presence in Washington. Many powerful and well-informed associations have their headquarters in Washington.

One example, when a commercial aircraft crash occurs, experienced Web users are able to go to sites to locate background information on the type of aircraft, and even recover maintenance records on the specific aircraft involved. Similarly, the Airline Pilots Association might post their commentary on the crash.

Reporter Diane Dimond, who cohosted a program on CNBC with Geraldo Rivera, used the Web when she was working on a syndicated program in Los Angeles to research a story about the military, acquiring information that would have been very difficult to obtain through traditional telephone research and in person interviews:

> While working at the syndicated news magazine *EXTRA* (Warner Brothers/ Telepictures) I did several reports in a series on veterans and Gulf War Illness. As

part of my follow ups I learned a lot about the Anthrax vaccination and its possible ill effects on veterans who took it during the Gulf war. After Defense Secretary Cohen announced recently that ALL members of the military would HAVE TO receive the 18 month long series of shots, I got to wondering how many soldiers and sailors didn't want to take something that was under such suspicion.

My producer and I hit the Internet and found MANY active duty sailors (serving on the U.S.S. INDEPENDENCE and on the U.S.S. STENNIS in the Persian Gulf) were already communicating among themselves and their families back home about their reluctance, actually their REFUSAL, to take the shots. As a result of contacting them on the Internet (and their families back stateside) we were able to orchestrate ship-to-shore telephone calls with so-called "refusers"—those sailors who were actively facing court martial and loss of benefits because they refused the shots. We realized we had uncovered a mini-mutiny at sea. After some of the sailors came home on leave we arranged via the Internet to meet them at their homes and do on-camera interviews. Coupled with the ship-to-shore phone calls we had recorded we had ourselves quite a good story. The Pentagon refused to comment on the growing rebellion at sea—and still does refuse to comment but we continue to stay in touch with the "REFUSERS" and many still fear retribution from the military. None of our refuser information could have been gathered without the Internet! (personal communication, August 5, 1998)

SPECIAL SITES FOR SPECIAL NEEDS

Experienced Internet users have favorite sites that they visit, either because they pick up story ideas and information they need or because they make frequent use of a site to flesh out news stories. There are programs available that allow you to arrange your favorite information sites in a logical order so that you can make quick daily sweeps to see if they have anything interesting. Newspapers all over the world have Web sites. One caution, some sites require subscription (they charge fees); others are free.

Sites Related to Ethics Issues

Two major journalists' organizations, the Society of Professional Journalists (SPJ; http://www.spj.org) and the Radio-Television News Directors Association (http://www.rtnda.org) are on the front line in discussions of journalistic ethics.

The nonprofit Poynter Institute in St. Petersburg, Florida is a primary source for information on ethics. It can be found at http://www.poynter.org.

If you dig a little deeper, you will find special ethics programs and ethics chairs at a number of journalism and communication schools.

Career-Related Sites

The sites that best suit students and recent graduates seeking information about scholarships, internships, and jobs are those of the Radio-Television News Directors Association and the Society of Professional Journalists. Each state has a state broadcasters' association. Check the association site for job listings in areas that interest you. The National Association of Broadcasters also has job-related information.

Job listings can be obtained through at http://www.tvspy.com. The RTNDA provides links, or you can seek directly other organizations involved in training and placement. The Radio and Television News Directors Foundation (RTNDF) supports in-service training programs. The e-mail addresses are rtnda@rtnda.org and rtndf@rtndf.org.

Some other helpful organizations include the Broadcasters Training Network, The Minorities in Broadcasting Training Program, and The Poynter Institute. Scholarship information can be obtained from the Broadcast Education Association.

Organizations that provide networks for particular groups of professionals include the Association for Women in Communication, the National Association of Black Journalists, the National Association of Hispanic Journalists, the Asian Journalists' Association, the South Asian Journalists' Association and the National Lesbian and Gay Journalists' Association.

CONCLUSION

Once you begin to explore (or surf) the Web, you may find it difficult to leave the keyboard. As a practical matter, many older journalists have not become comfortable with the e-mail and Web surfing, which will give you an opportunity to show what you can do. There is, however, an increasing assumption among news managers that younger people coming to work in the newsroom probably know quite a bit about the Internet. It's quite likely someone will assume you know what you are doing and ask you to do a web search. It's best to be prepared!

One caveat: Web surfing does not replace the fundamentals of good journalism, such as making phone calls, attending meetings, and conducting in-person interviews. Most of all, the accuracy of information retrieved from the Web needs to be cross-checked, as not all sources have proven reliable.

9
Managing a Computerized Newsroom

Installing specialized computer systems in broadcast newsrooms has created employment opportunities for recent college graduates who are computer literate and comfortable with software. Most broadcast newsroom computer systems are large enough to require having at least one person on staff with advanced training to deal with system management, maintenance and security. Many broadcast newsrooms maintain Web sites on the Internet that require personnel and upkeep. Veteran newsroom employees may not have the in-depth knowledge of desktop computing or the interest that is required for system and Web site management, thus creating opportunities for younger, more computer-literate journalists.

An employee of Turner Broadcasting volunteered to work with the CNN newsroom computer system when it was first being installed. There weren't many CNN news staff members who saw any future in computers in 1980, but Rob Barnes endured all the hardships of developing something new and went on to become the head of all news computing activities for Turner Broadcasting before moving directly into an executive position in the computer industry.

SYSTEM OPERATOR: SUPER-USER

Computerization of broadcast newsrooms has created two types of newsroom jobs, system operators and Web site editors. The larger newsroom computer systems (40–100 terminals) require the services of at least one person to train others and troubleshoot when users run into problems. Two important operational concerns are keeping enough unused capacity in the system so that it will not freeze up and maintaining security so the news department's files don't have unwanted visitors.

The system operator may have to respond to pager calls at odd hours, but as a result, the system operator has much higher visibility throughout the organization. System operators have gone on to work as operations managers, information system managers, and Web site editors. Others have gotten on a fast track to become producers. One reason this happens is that producers use computers in their daily routine, another is that the super-user has an overview of everything that is happening.

One way to prepare yourself for the responsibilities of operating a computer system is to become as computer-literate as possible in relation to the computer technology you are currently using. Many personal computer users learn what they need to know to use their computer without thoroughly studying their hardware or software instruction manuals. Reading and learning the functions of the PC through manuals, or good, independently written books are first steps to becoming proficient with computers.

A good computer system operator knows all of the functions of the operating system (DOS and Windows-NT® are starting points), as well as all the capabilities of the software. Avail yourself of any chance to get advanced training, either in college classes, or through employer training programs. The newsroom computer firms that install large, complex systems usually have advanced training seminars available for system operators. Employers frequently subsidize this advanced level training if a computer-literate employee makes a strong case that the additional training will help to avoid computer down time and increase staff utilization of the system.

Lee Perryman, the Deputy Director, Broadcast Services and Director of Broadcast Technology for the Associated Press, described the training his company gives customers of the AP's electronic news production system:

FIG. 9.1. A typical Associated Press ENPS screen. Photo courtesy AP/ENPS.

As part of every ENPS installation, AP's broadcast technology group provides advanced training to newsroom computer "Super Users." It is recommended that the news organization select for those roles not just technically oriented members of the news or engineering staffs but at least one person whose primary orientation is editorial. It is only with an editorial side "advocate" in the newsroom that people will continue to grow in their system capabilities. (personal communication, August 15, 1998)

Perryman said computer literacy is important for journalism students in getting a job:

There are a couple of levels to this ... first, for more technically oriented people, they can move into a news operations position (an assignment editor, for instance) in which they might be responsible for a variety of technical issues including newsroom computer supervision, live shots, gear, etc. More and more of what those folks do is dependent on computer knowledge.

More important, though, in my view are journalists who, while understanding the technical issues of computers, can translate that knowledge into changes and configurations that can benefit the journalist in the newsroom. This involves an ability to think critically about "how" things get done in the broadcast news operation, and to evaluate how a computer system can change or improve those work practices.

Frankly, for those who want to get the technical background, the Web can provide almost anything they need. Especially valuable are some of the Microsoft sites that have detailed articles on networking and other technical issues. There are also many sites with glossaries of computer terms, etc.

Perryman urged entry-level newsroom employees to learn all they could by working with the system, reading on their own, and "shadowing" the news organization's current system-super user or system administrator.

One of the key duties of a system super-user is to develop training programs for the newsroom staff. Turnover tends to be high in the news business, and new staff members must be introduced to the news system quickly, so they can log on and get into a daily work mode. Usually, the initial training is very simple and functional, designed to get an employee working on a terminal. Later, it may be desirable to do further training to demonstrate how the system can help an employee with less routine tasks, such as Internet research. Staff members moving to the assignment desk or to producer slots need additional training on the system in order to use its special functions.

The super-user also plays an important role in preserving security for the system. No news operation wants outside individuals looking through its files, or worse, disrupting its system. The system operator is responsible for establishing and enforcing security procedures, as well as conducting checks to make certain no one has breached the system's security.

A parallel problem is the introduction of *viruses,* or rogue computer programs into the system. These can damage files and stop the system. The system operator helps establish antivirus procedures and performs virus checks on the system. One chief engineer went so far as to disable all floppy disk units on his news department's computers because viruses are frequently, usually unwittingly, introduced from computer disks that are brought into the newsroom by employees.

JOBS FOR PEOPLE WHO HAVE COMPUTER SKILLS

There are a variety of jobs available to broadcast journalists who have advanced knowledge of computers and software.

Video Editor. Some industry observers point to a trend to combine more tasks as the reporter/writer's desk, including editing news tape. Our view is that low-skill video editors, people who do the simpler sorts of news tape editing, may find fewer opportunities as time goes by. Much of the simple voice-over editing will move out of the news edit suite and onto reporter/writer terminals. Very sophisticated editing, the sort done for ratings period features, promotional announcements, investigative reports, documentaries, and postproduction of network programs, is a creative skill for which employers will pay handsomely. If you want to go into video editing, learn as much as you can, attend vendor and industry training sessions and study the work of the masters.

Computer Industry/Business Reporter. An increasing number of reporters are specializing in topics related to computers and the computer industry. Computers will be part of our lives for decades, so reporters who can explain how computers work or who can track the computer industry are going to be in demand.

Producer. Any television producer needs to be able to get the most out of the organization's computer system. Producers who can do Internet searches to develop new background information or news stories are in demand. Producers have to know their systems because they are the first people to be called on when someone in the newsroom is having difficulty with a computer.

Assignment Editor. Assignment editors depend a great deal on computers, to help them search for records and information, manage crews and assignments, to relay messages, and to keep track of contacts.

Satellite Coordinator. Many stations have a designated coordinator or producer who is in charge of keeping track of all incoming and outgoing satellite feeds. In some stations this could amount to 300 or more individual story offerings per day. The satellite coordinator keeps specialized information on a terminal and has frequent contact with the assignment desk and broadcast producers. This position, frequently one step above assistant producer, has been a successful launching

FIG. 9.2. Newsroom automation terminals are found in control rooms. Producers and directors use them to follow the run sheet and make last-minute adjustments in the program's running order. Photo courtesy of AP/ENPS.

point for behind-the-scenes careers. Experience as a satellite coordinator has particular relevance to networks and satellite cooperatives.

Promotion Producer. This is a "hot" field. Good promotion producers who can take a current news story and quickly turn out audience-attracting promos are in demand. Almost every broadcast/cable news organization employs people who create instant promotions for use on air. A promotion producer has to be able to recognize a news story, especially one that is being handled skillfully by the news department. The news promo producer uses the newsroom computer system to check on what is being done, what is planned, and what sort of coverage is scheduled. Promotion producers also have to write compelling copy with severe time restrictions. Most positions require the producer to be able to edit on the latest digital editing devices.

Webmaster/Web Producer. Another "hot" job and a good career starter for broadcast journalists. News organizations at every level have established or are setting up Web sites. The strength of many of these sites is local news copy. Newsroom computer system vendors now include Internet software in their packages, including software that transfers the news program script (and in some cases, audio and video) to the Web page. Major networks not only send their scripts, they create additional information for viewers who want to know more about a current topic.

Web page designers and writer/editors are in demand. Most older staff members are not familiar with Web software, and so younger journalists have a major opportunity. Overall maintenance and design of the Web page is another concern in news organizations. You can't have a stale Web site if you are going to tell everyone they are getting the latest news.

Researcher. Many journalism students miss an opportunity by not checking into researcher positions. Large news organizations and syndicators of news-related programming employ many college graduates to perform all kinds of research tasks. The risk of lawsuits alone is sufficient to encourage major news organizations to check every fact in their prime-time news programs. Researchers play a major role in investigative reporting and in election coverage. Computer skills are a must in this field!

System Manager. Newsroom computer automation systems represent major investments for media companies, and it is important that they be kept running efficiently. Many news organizations employ at least one person to supervise the system. This involves trouble-shooting, training, file clean-out and management, software upgrades, hardware and software expenditure recommendations, and maintenance of internal and external system security. Many news organizations prefer to employ system managers who have journalistic training. They usually subsidize super-user and advanced super-user training at vendor sites, which increases the system manager's importance in the organization.

THE WEB SITE

News-based Web sites have become important sources of information during times of heightened news interest. CNN.com drew 3,400,000 visitors at its site on September 11, 2002, the anniversary of the destruction of the World Trade Center and the attack on the Pentagon. That represented a 49% increase over CNN.com's average Wednesday traffic. MSNBC.com had 2,596,000 visitors, up 43%.[1]

News organizations use Web sites for two reasons, to match the competition and to provide an additional revenue stream by reprocessing information the organization has already acquired. Web site production offers excellent opportunities for computer and Internet literate journalists. In some organizations, Web sites are becoming a training ground for writers.

Many television news organizations use special software to pull news broadcast scripts from their newsroom computer system, and send the script directly to a Web

---

[1] API Roundtable. Friday, October 4, 2002.

MANAGING A COMPUTERIZED NEWSROOM 149

FIG. 9.3. New technology is always arriving in the newsroom. This wireless computer-tablet can be loaded with either the rundown or the script, allowing a director to "mark up" a script with a stylus, just as she would have marked a paper script using a pen. In general, directors like to work from a printed page, which this computer mimics. Photo courtesy of Autocue Systems Inc.

site. It costs news organizations very little to add Internet service since the major expense of newsgathering has been absorbed by on-air broadcasts.

Local news, weather, sports, and other information can be extracted from data already in the newsroom computer. Audio and video can be fed via a telephone modem or the faster broadband services. Many sites are transmitting video, it's called *video streaming*. Video streaming requires a great deal of *bandwidth* or data capacity. Telephone carriers and cable companies are offering wide-band, high-speed services at a premium. Telephone companies frequently call these services *DSL* for digital subscriber lines, and cable company frequently refer to their service as *digital cable modems*.

One of the selling points of news organizations is news. This is why Web sites require producers, editors, and writers to provide additional information, beyond the brief items typically broadcast as television news stories. The station Web site can publish video that hasn't been used on broadcasts. The Web staff can provide additional details in text form, or supplement a story with charts or feature material.

Web site personnel can collect community information such as the city recreation department schedule and scores from amateur athletic leagues. Some television stations subscribe to content services that provide national or generic content that is integrated into the local Web site.

Web site consultants consistently say that people go to Web sites for information, especially news. Some say a news organization site should be able to staff breaking news, which attracts viewers to the Web pages.

MULTIMEDIA

One of the challenges facing television news departments is training reporters to prepare special Web versions of their stories. In a world that is increasingly emphasizing multimedia, reporters, writers, videographers, and producers need to be able to cross disciplines. For example, WMTW-TV in Portland, Maine operated a television station, a Web site, and several radio stations (including all-news radio) in the same market. There is increasing need for radio and TV reporters to prepare items for the Web. Another challenge the station had not fully addressed during a visit in 2001 was training reporters and producers to write for all three media: television, all-news radio, and the Web. The three divisions were sharing information over the phone and by e-mail, but newsgathering personnel were not fully crosstrained in multimedia news.

The *Florida Times-Union* newspaper in Jacksonville has trained some newspaper reporters to be television reporters. Their video stories are carried on the newspaper's Web site and some appear on a Jacksonville television station.

Media General Corporation has one of the most sophisticated multimedia operations in the United States in Tampa, Florida. The company's daily newspaper, *The Tampa Tribune;* television station, WFLA-TV; and Web site, Tampa Bay Online (TBO.com) all operate from the same facility that was built specifically to house several media newsrooms. Reporters and photographers work across the media outlets.

The *Orlando Sentinel* in Orlando, Florida has a fairly sophisticated Web site, with an experienced news director/producer in charge. The newspaper's photographers shoot still pictures and video and reporters are expected to be able to do a television version of their story. The video goes on the newspaper Web site, and some is run on a regional all-news cable channel. The development of the *Sentinel* video Web site created several new positions for people with video journalism backgrounds.

A large Internet news organization is CNN Interactive (www.cnn.com or www.cnnfn.com). It is advertiser supported and sells specialized services to customers within the CNN family and to external clients. CNN provides low-resolution video to subscribers.

PROMOTION

Web sites also act as promotional vehicles for the main TV news activity such as a station's news broadcasts. They crossrefer readers to news video, weather forecasts, and sports information. The Web site usually lists the times of news broadcasts, it features pictures of on-air personalities and provides links to special services, such as consumer problem solving, offered by the TV station.

Another service is providing daily news summaries by e-mail to a list of subscribers. These can be very handy for busy computer users and are a great promotional tool. Web site information can be delivered to some cellphones and personal data assistants (PDAs).

TOOLS FOR NEWS DIRECTORS

The fact that most newsroom computer systems are built around personal computers gives the news director the opportunity of using the computer system for functions that are exclusive to the duties of the department manager.

Most systems are set up so a manager can use special spreadsheet or budget software on a system terminal. The system contains safeguards that permit the news manager to lock out access to files if they are not intended to be viewed by the news staff. The main advantage to this arrangement is that the news manager does not have to have an additional terminal in the office.

News managers can also use their access to the computer system to monitor closely the activities of the newsroom staff. The manager can bring up news copy, assignment sheets and producer rundowns on an office terminal, permitting the manager to watch the work that is being produced without having to walk to the newsroom or interfere with an employee's workflow.

The news manager can go into the early- and late-planning meetings briefed on what is going on, which is a decided advantage because one of a news manager's responsibilities is shaping the overall content and style of the news broadcasts.

News managers can use the computer system to send individual or group memos, which save a lot of time and paper. David Baer, station manager and news director at WMTW-TV in Portland, Maine, liked to provide his comments on the station's news broadcasts via e-mail. The executive producer monitored message traffic, and acted immediately on Baer's suggestions. WMTW had a lean staff, and e-mail critiques were more efficient than trying to hold over the production and news staffs for the early evening news block in order to hold a live meeting. Baer provided comments on the 11 p.m. and weekend news blocks from his home terminal.

One of the tasks a news manager faces is responding to management questions about the background of stories, or discrepancies or errors in stories. The archives system, the wire files, the producer rundowns, and assignment desk information can be checked for information. This sort of check may resolve an issue. If not, it may save the news manager time when he or she has to talk with specific staff members in order to gather information to respond to a management memo.

It is frequently possible to interface the news manager's terminal to the traffic automation system and an internal message network for special applications that apply only to management issues.

Some software permits news managers to do some analysis within the system. A typical concern might be the amount of *face-time* (on camera appearance time) a certain anchor was getting in a program. The news director could research any claims of imbalance prior to having to discuss the issue with news anchors or their agents.

Another analysis might break out figures on story subjects, or localities, or the balance between on-camera and voice-over stories.

Managers in news organizations spend a great deal of time dealing with scheduling issues. Most newsroom systems provide areas within the system to keep personnel information, such as vacation schedules, as well as providing an organized format for keeping and disseminating staff schedules. The system manager, working with news executives, defines what portion of the scheduling software is available to the whole staff, and what portion is locked out of general access.

Another important personnel issue is overtime. A manager can isolate overtime from other expenses, and research the reasons for the additional costs. This information is important for budget planning and is essential to any effort to control costs.

Most news managers rely heavily on their desktop terminals for internal and external correspondence, monitoring industry news, checking on possible new hires, and keeping up their contacts within the business. A news director who is considering hiring an anchorperson from another station may watch that station's streaming video. This has the advantage of allowing the news manager to observe a potential anchor on a live broadcast, rather than trying to judge how that person will function on-air, based on a prerecorded audition tape. Computer-based correspondence has become a useful alternative to meetings and telephone conference calls.

Another use for the manager's computer is to access information from vendors who supply programming and technical equipment. Illustrations, catalogues and specification sheets are almost universally available on vendor Web sites. The news manager who finds that the budget is too tight to support a trip to an industry convention, such as the Radio-TV News Directors Association conference or the National Association of Broadcasters convention can access both vendor information and convention sessions via Web sites.

CONCLUSION

The newsroom computer system has taken on such an important role in news organizations that it's very existence has created new positions for people who are willing to learn a little more than average about the capabilities and operation of a sophisticated networked computer automation system.

10
Bells and Whistles

Newsrooms and their systems come in various shapes and sizes. The requirements of a large network organization differ significantly from the requirements of a medium-market television station. In this chapter we discuss the special features of very large news operations and newsroom automation systems.

THE REALLY, REALLY BIG SYSTEM

Network-type newsgathering organizations have their own unique requirements for newsroom operations. A major priority is dealing with the matter of communication. How do you connect hundreds, even thousands, of journalists and managers so that they share information they need but not information (personnel records or equipment inventories) they don't need? What can be done so that journalists benefit from the newsgathering capabilities of a large organization?

A major business theme today is the creation of a large pool of raw stories (video, audio, text) that can be accessed by anyone in the organization, and reshaped for distribution by several different media or media outlets, such as conventional television, cable television, airport monitors, Web sites, cellular telephones, radio networks, and foreign language broadcasts. This approach is called *asset management*. Raw video is stored in computer servers that are connected to a computer network. This permits several users to simultaneously withdraw the same video, and edit their own story versions from the tape that was shot in the field, or downloaded from an external source. A sophisticated computer system is required to accomplish these tasks.

CNN

The founders of the Cable News Network realized in 1977, when they were putting together the network, that new technology would be needed if they were going to establish what was then the fourth TV network news organization. Ted Turner's management team looked at every possible way to keep costs down while competing against the quality of the Big 3 networks (ABC, CBS, NBC). At the time, Turner said he expected to commit $100 million to CNN before it became profitable. By comparison, the Big 3 networks were spending more than $100 million *annually* on their news divisions.[1]

At the time automation was not a major cost saver for terrestrial TV broadcasters. It was decided that a newsroom computer system could save a large amount of money CNN would have had to spend on Teletype paper. A computer system would also allow CNN to reuse or reprocess a story. As it turned out, the latter idea proved to be the real money saver because each additional use of material could generate income without adding significantly to the cost of newsgathering.

Former CNN Director of Data Processing Robert Barnes said CNN picked the BASYS newsroom computer company because Peter Kolstad and Ed Grudzien, its partners, "had the most realistic viewpoint on what needed to be done and how to handle it" (P. Kolstad, personal communication, September 23, 1980). Kolstad and Grudzien had already invested 3 years in developing a basic system. In 1980, they spent several months in an uncomfortable room in the old CNN building in Atlanta building CNN's newsroom computer system to specifications everyone hoped would be workable.

The system was phased in late in 1980. Kolstad (personal communication, September 23, 1980) described the early CNN system as: "A big wire service reader and a sort of message handler." Ted Kavanau (personal communication, September 23, 1980), who was a senior news producer at the time, said the system also listed satellite news feeds.

The daring gamble on computer technology worked well enough for CNN, and when CNN Headline News was created, BASYS was asked to build a newsroom computer system for the new channel. It made production of the news much more efficient.

Although still struggling to earn revenue and establish itself as a legitimate news organization, CNN became the destination for leaders of other news organizations that were trying to determine what technology could do for them. What these news executives saw at CNN led to the installation of newsroom computer systems at the British Broadcasting Corporation and Independent Television News, both in London.

CNN is committed to using computer automation technology to write, edit, and produce the news. CNN installed the most advanced AvidiNews system.[2] Avid Technologies bought BASYS and practically redesigned the system to meet newer automation and digital technology demands, which meant that producers and writers had to learn new systems.

---

[1] Press release. *CNN Upgrades to AvidNews Computer System*. Tewksbury, MA: Avid Corporation. July 13, 1998.

[2] These issues were introduced in the Home Office White Paper, "Broadcasting in the '90s: Competition, choice and quality," November, 1988, and were further enunciated when the BBC Charter was renewed in 1996.

FIG. 10.1. An editor at work on a Media-100 system. Photo courtesy of Media 100 Inc.

The AvidiNews system installed at CNN/US; CNNfn; CNN International and Headline news resulted in upgrading 1,300 workstations. The workstations deliver text, video, and audio to the journalists' desks. Avid said the new system allowed CNN journalists, editors, producers and news directors to share and access video, scripts and rundowns. CNN staffers can publish news stories in the HTML format on the World Wide Web at www.CNN.com. CNN has layers and levels of producers for every service it offers.

One of the remarkable achievements of communication technology is that the Tokyo bureau of a major network has the same networked newsroom computer technology as the network headquarters, therefore the bureau staff has access to the same information as journalists in the central newsroom. This permits more frequent and faster communication and results in closer ties between the bureau and network central. It is much easier to coordinate information using data channels and text messages, compared to making overseas telephone calls, which were subject to delays, disconnection and distortion.

CNN's objective in its upgrade was to make its tremendous inventory of current and past video available in digital form, so that a journalist could retrieve video the same way a news script was accessed. The master copies of the video would be held on computers called *servers* and any editing suite or workstation would be able to withdraw a copy of the video and edit it to meet specialized needs. The edited piece would become a separate file, which would be returned to a server until it was withdrawn so it could be placed in the lineup to be played as part of a CNN broadcast. With Headline News broadcasting 24 hours a day, the producers needed to have the ability to access file tape for reworking to keep their broadcasts fresh and interesting.

We visited CNN headquarters in Atlanta to observe the network's producers and learn how newsroom automation was used by CNN. The program being prepared was the 4:00 to 4:30 p.m. network news broadcast, *CNN TODAY,* for the main CNN News channel.

The program team was led by an executive producer who was assisted by a producer. Both worked in small areas in the open main newsroom. Each had a desktop computer terminal. CNN producers could access a lot of information by searching the Web on their system terminals as well as CNN-Interactive, the CNN Internet service. They also used archive background material and CNN's own archives for transcripts of current stories. CNN has an enormous daily inventory of video and packaged stories that is accessible to any of its networks, including CNN, Headlines News, Airport News, CNN-Financial News, CNN International, CNN Spanish, and CNN Interactive.

When the desired video came up on the producer's screen, the producer saw the transcript in one window, with time code in and time code out information (to help select edit-points), as well as running time, and the video in another. Time code is imbedded on most videotapes made in the United States under a system devised by SMPTE, the Society of Motion Picture and Television Engineers. Video editing equipment will read out the clock time imbedded on the recorded track, and any point on the tape or disk can be identified by the time readout. This is essential to videotape or digital media editing.

There was also a "tapes alert file," which producers checked for anticipated materials.

The CNN broadcast was slotted for 8 minutes of commercials. The length of the segments was flexible, and the producers tried to reserve about 1:30 at the end of the broadcast for the anchors to come back and lead into the next program.

Graphics requests were filed using an order form available on the terminal screen. The graphics staff was located on another floor in the CNN Center. One disadvantage to this arrangement, according to producers, was less personal contact with the graphics specialists. Producers would occasionally get up and walk to other areas in order to talk to production people or writers.

Daily editorial meetings were held at 8:30 a.m. and 2:30 p.m. The typical staffing for a CNN News broadcast was:

Executive Producer

Producer

Associate Producer: pulled tapes, viewed raw tape, handled the tape lineup at playback.

Copy Editor

Writers: 1 or 2 full-time and a third, for 2 hours.

Washington producer—worked with several programs.

Interactive Producer

Auxiliary services including tape feeds, tape editing, and graphics. These units serviced the whole organization.

The executive producer arrived at CNN Center at 7:30 a.m. to "read in" before the 8:30 a.m. editorial meeting to get an overview of what was going on. The executive producer was also assigned to produce any breaking news until 5 p.m. (If a hot new story broke, the executive producer on duty would be responsible for getting it on and off the air.) The 4 p.m. producer covered from 5 to 6 p.m.

THE PRELIMINARY RUNDOWN FOR 4 P.M.

Section 1: Clinton sex scandal, Lewinsky.

[Live report by Wolf Blitzer from White House.]

Section 2: Cuba—Pope John Paul II visit.

Yassir Arafat visits Washington.

UN Disarmament leader—UN Inspection Chief Richard Butler on Iraq and "weapons of mass destruction."

Kasi sentenced—man who murdered two CIA employees outside CIA headquarters gets death sentence.

Section 3: Weather and Health stories (weather was done live from a special studio).

Health stories were: flu in United States, Hong Kong Bird flu (killing chickens) and UK story on mad cow disease.

Section 4: Mainly business news originating from CNN-fn (financial news) in New York.

Section 5: Shuttle launch from Florida today.

There was a news staff meeting 3 hours before the broadcast (1 p.m.) with the writers, the copy editor, and the associate producer. This sort of national broadcast was set up to react to change as stories break. Rundowns frequently changed during the broadcast.

In addition to the rundown the computer screens have vast lists of video and summaries of their content. It was interesting to note that despite these resources, producers still relied on their memories to recall sources of archive video—or information about stories. CNN is continuing to invest in archives technology to simplify storage and retrieval of video.

At 2:53 p.m. the executive producer was notified he had lost the use of Wolf Blitzer to do a live cut-in on the White House scandal. His superior came over to the desk and told him. Blitzer had been given 4 minutes, so the producers had to decide what to do to fill the time. They put writers to work on a substitute story using a large stock of available video and sound-on-tape (SOT) on the White House story.

In talking to writers the executive producer said: "Let's start strong and get personal ..." describing the type of content he wanted covering the scandal in which President Clinton was accused of having sex with a White House intern named Monica Lewinsky.

The producer for the Cuba remote (Pope's visit) came by. The broadcast producers decided to toss the story to correspondent Christiane Amanpour who would be live from Cuba. She would introduce correspondent Brent Sadler on tape, then Amanpour would do a question and answer section with the broadcast's two anchors. They decide to slightly expand the time allotted to coverage of the Pope in Cuba. This day the Pope had gone to preach in another city (other than Havana) in Cuba.

At 3:05 p.m. the producer walked across the newsroom to talk to the anchors. The executive producer had already sent a written message to the anchors, using a one-line message writing function that displayed on the top of the computer screen. The executive producer also messaged a number of people that the show was losing Blitzer and wrote a protest note to his superiors.

The pace accelerated quickly starting at 3:05 p.m., partly due to the loss of the live appearance by the White House correspondent. By this time, the executive producer was busy on the terminal used for preparation of the actual producer rundown. This was because with an all-news entity like CNN, rundowns constantly change.

Both producers were writing, mostly transitions and short anchor pieces or VOs (voiceovers), which would be held to make up time if necessary, otherwise they would be dropped. Once they were done writing, the copy was automatically sent to the rundown. The scripts were typed in the middle of the screen, with video on the left. Many television news departments simply split the screen roughly in half, typing video information on the left, and copy on the right.

The producer reported the Brent Sadler piece from Cuba did not come in on time at 3:15 on the satellite feed and was not yet in house. An associate producer was working on coordinating the coverage from Cuba. At 3:35 Cuba was not locked up.

The producer walked downstairs to get the graphics for the broadcast.

Havana fed the Sadler piece at 3:38 p.m.

At 3:42 the executive producer went over the program's list of tapes with the director.

At 3:44 p.m. the executive producer asked: "Are we OK?" The producer said: "I think so." The producers were viewing the feed of the Sadler piece from Cuba. They were informed Sadler ran 2:21.

At 3:51 p.m. six items were showing question marks on producer screen—they were not fully checked and approved.

At 3:55 p.m. the executive producer and producer walked to a nearby control room. The executive producer sat in the chair next to the director and technical director (switcher). The producer sat at a desk on the rear tier and watched time and setups for live shots, among other duties. Both had terminals at their positions.

There were nine people in the control room plus two anchors in the studio. Two young women sat at the graphics console operating the character generator because some of the CGs might be changed during the program. Character generators can be automated but usually require an operator if the broadcast anticipates many late changes.

The female anchor's mike battery died, and a quick switch was made.

The meteorologist came up live from another studio at the end of the preceding program. The weather brief was followed by a live report from CNN Financial News in New York. (The financial news script was prepared on newsroom computer terminals in New York and became part of the central file, available to any CNN location.) The business report ran over. Because cable, unlike licensed broadcast stations, does not have to comply with federal regulations about identifying the source of a broadcast *exactly* on the hour, time is not as important at it would be at a broadcast network.

The broadcast began at 4:00:29.

The director was working from paper scripts that were written on the computer system, and printed out as well as being saved to the producer rundown. New pages kept being delivered by a production assistant. The rundown was up on terminal screens The computer system corrected story entries and times as new scripts were entered from terminals. The executive producer called for a change of graphics.

The Cuba producer was talking on two telephones simultaneously, coordinating with the crew and Christiane Amanpour in Cuba. Some aspects of news production still need the immediacy of direct verbal contact. There was a discussion about a dropped line of copy on page 11, which producers in Cuba and Atlanta could read on their screens. Cuba, on the phone and an audio feed, said the controversy mentioned in the copy was not as strong as originally thought, the copy needed to be changed.

CNN shipped 32 terminals to Cuba for the Pope's visit. They were fed to modems with four devices to a modem. The modems were connected to ordinary dial-up telephone lines. Some of the terminals were laptop computers.

A visual was dropped from the lineup.

While the Cuba live feed was underway the executive producer and the producer were discussing yesterday's ratings, which were circulated as a staff message in the newsroom messaging area of the terminal screens. (CNN TODAY had gotten a 1.5 rating, about 1,122,000 U.S. homes, the previous afternoon due to Pope in Cuba and Clinton-Lewinsky scandal coverage.)

4:14:59: out of the satellite feed from Cuba. Amanpour's live report ran 5 minutes. The anchors joined at the end to do a live question and answer session with Amanpour. (The anchors, associate producer and Amanpour discussed the content of the reports from Cuba so the anchor questions would make sense and not repeat something covered in some other portion of the live feed.)

At 4:20 Amanpour is live again, this time on CNN-International. The control room can monitor all CNN channels. The producer suggested killing the *Day in History* feature to make up time, the executive producer agrees, someone says it was weak anyway. The remainder of the broadcast went according to the plan described on the rundown.

CNN Director of News Technology, Gina Gershon, said producers played a very important role during the development of AvidiNews automation by describing what they needed to see and use on their terminals. Computer programmers needed to know the nature of the work flow at a producer's desk, who approved scripts, and what sort of check-off (approval) system producers needed in order to be certain no unapproved copy or stories got on the air. Another important issue was deciding on the type of timing system producers wished to use.

One problem at CNN is that it goes live frequently for extended periods, and this puts a great deal of strain on the automation system.

Trainers at CNN said journalists learned the system quicker if they were familiar with computers loaded with Windows® software. Writers could be trained quickly because they did not need to know many functions in order to do their work.

Producers had to learn how to build a rundown, timing, and how to print scripts and rundowns (G. Gershon, personal communication, January 23, 1998).

The major difference in CNN's operation and those of the older New York networks is that at CNN the majority of the incoming material flows into a giant video pool, from which producers in the various services may draw. The newsroom computer system is critical to keeping track of this inventory, and with the addition of viewing capability at terminals, producers have better control over quality and content. The New York networks frequently assign correspondents and crews to stories to cover for a specific broadcast. While the 4 p.m. CNN TODAY broadcast got some priority treatment in terms of access to live coverage from Cuba, the crew in Cuba fed several other live shots to other broadcasts, with very little time between each feed.

Most of the information flow in the CNN newsroom moves via computer terminals. It is simply too large an area to allow shouting across the room, especially because the on-air studio is adjacent. CNN and CNN International together could be seen in 184 million households in 210 countries and territories.

THE BBC

The British Broadcasting Corporation is enormous. It is a semiautonomous government nonprofit corporation, supported by taxes on television receivers, grants, and the sale of its programming outside Britain. It provides national radio, television and cable/satellite (all-news) network programming to England, Scotland, Ulster (Northern Ireland), and Wales. It does a huge amount of international broadcasting using short-wave radio and satellite radio and television. The BBC also operates local radio and television stations in the United Kingdom. The BBC operates teletext (text on television screens) and Internet services. The BBC is major producer of programs, including current affairs (which U.S. broadcasters call *public affairs*).

In the mid-1990s BBC News and Current Affairs was faced with two significant concerns. Changes in the broadcasting law and in the economic structure of the British government were putting pressure on the Corporation. Meanwhile, the British taxpayer was balking at the rising cost of the television receiver tax. By 1995 there were calls for the BBC to both cut its government funded operating budget, and develop additional ways to earn money.[3]

To News and Current Affairs, this meant do more with less, and make the best use of resources. As discussions went on, technology began to be seen as offering some solutions. One solution that had already been tried was the use of virtual technology to create sets for news broadcasts. BBC Television had been using a version of this technology on its 1 p.m. weekday national broadcast for several years. The news anchor sat at a real desk, but the backgrounds were supplied from electronic graphics devices, using the same techniques that are used for weather forecasts. The audience at home saw the newscaster and the background, but spectators in the studio viewing room saw that there was nothing behind the news anchor, except a neutral background. All the lights, texture, color and images were inserted from a graphics device.

The cost saving was in not having to construct an expensive set and not having to take down and set up a set for each broadcast. Many TV studios are used for several broadcasts, and between the broadcasts, stage crews come in and change the backgrounds, move furniture, refocus lights, and install microphones.

Virtual technology goes beyond creating just a background. A graphics computer can create the appearance of a three-dimensional set where none exists. It is a tricky technology, but once the performers and technical crew become accustomed to its peculiarities, all that is required to get a set ready is a series of commands to a computer.

The BBC had been in the forefront of developing virtual studio technology, and it was integrated into some news presentations as a way to lower costs. The BBC had used newsroom computer technology since 1982, mainly for word processing and archiving. It was decided, in the mid-1990s, that the scattered newsroom computer systems, some obsolete, others part of the third BASYS system ever built, needed to be updated or replaced. What was needed was a sophisticated computer system that could bring together the vast newsgathering resources of the BBC while

---

[3]The author inspected the first BBC BASYS system in January, 1983. It was installed in late 1982 but union negotiations delayed its daily use until 1983. The author, at the same time, discussed a television newsroom computer system under development with the head of MIS services at BBC Television in White City.

FIG. 10.2. The British Broadcasting Corporation (BBC) produces 30 hours of children's programs every day for distribution over a variety of delivery channels. Autocue Ltd. adapted its newsroom computer technology to meet the complex scheduling tasks, as well as scriptwriting needs of CBBC. Notice that the computer is an off-the-shelf PC. Photo courtesy of Autocue, Ltd.

offering wage savings through automation of studio production and shifting news story production to the journalists' workstations.

The News and Current Affairs (NCA) managers knew they had some of the world's finest resources, but communication among the parts was primitive or nonexistent. They also knew that the highly structured, union-based workforce was going to have to be trimmed and a concept called *multiskilling*, where people are trained to perform several types of tasks, was going to have to be introduced.

A count of wire services going into the newsroom computer system showed 24 wires in News and Current Affairs at TV Centre, 16 wires each at network radio, 16 wires at World Service, and 12 wires in regional newsrooms. These figures demon-

BELLS AND WHISTLES 163

strate just how difficult it was for producers to monitor input as most of the wires came in on paper.

The system the BBC proposed involved new concepts. It was developed in conjunction with the Associated Press and named the Electronic News Production System or ENPS. As the name implies, producers and the production of news broadcasts were the paramount elements. The BBC had enough money, energy, patience, and resolve to get what it required, rather than settling for an existing system "package." The proposal combined features in use in other systems, plus a long list of items managers and journalists wanted added.

Some of the functions the system was required to provide included:

Wires: Available on computer screens, including financial tables, text, sound, video and stills.

Producer Running Orders: display at least four on one screen. Running order timings.

Scripts: with insertion of cues for automation.

Personal File Storage.

Messaging: single line messaging in real time and BBC wide e-mail capable of attaching data for graphics, video, audio, text to a message.

Information Organization: "folders" for users, some public, some private.

Foreign Language Support: at least 41 languages.

Information Distribution: news rundowns, messages, access to schedules, and so forth.

Search Facilities: ability to search a multimedia archive using a variety of search techniques.

User Profiles: a user defines what the terminal should look like and do, and that profile follows the user from terminal to terminal (a radio writer needs a different screen layout from a TV producer).

Users had to be able to access wires, scripts, running orders and messages in real-time, no matter where they were located. There were pages of detailed requirements relating to interfaces with various peripherals and interfaces for automation purposes. The automation interfaces included character generators, prompters, video monitors, machine control, robotic cameras, and playback from video and audio servers.

The development of ENPS marked a new stage in the development of broadcast newsroom computers.

The major differences in working in a large news organization are:

1. Specialization: tasks are more individualized, and each journalist is held to a higher quality standard. (This translates to: you don't make mistakes.)

2. More levels of supervision and more checks and balances.
3. Much of the organization's work centers on taking stories reported by someone else, and refining and polishing them to fit a distribution channel's requirements.
4. Significant reliance on computers for communication and research, rather than personal interaction.
5. Strict adherence to standards and procedures, offset by opportunities and resources for great creativity.

A journalist's job is narrowly defined and the computer system plays an important role by making possible the sharing of information and resources by a production team.

In a network newsroom, a writer may spend the working day writing at a terminal. Large news organizations have greater resources and they want their product—the script or news broadcast—to look and sound unique. This is accomplished by rewriting and editing and by having as much source material available to writers as possible. The BBC designed its system to handle a very large number of press agency wires, as well as news stories submitted by all of its own journalists, BBC stations, bureaus, and divisions. ENPS was designed to permit a journalist to type a keyword or highlight a phrase on a wire item, then click the *briefing* button. The system almost instantly tells the journalist everything it knows about stories, scripts, feeds, archives, expert contacts, and library clips relating to the briefing topic. This is valuable because speed is essential in most broadcast news applications. "Get it right and get it fast" is apt to be the motto in this type of organization.

Once a writer has reviewed the briefing list, the writer can use the computer's mouse to drag and drop text, audio, or video to a script.

While the writer types, a spell checker, a thesaurus, and a pronunciation guide provide backup. Scripts are timed and saved automatically. The writer can switch to a *template* (a fill-in-the-blank-form) to create character generator subtitles.

The script the writer creates is electronically transferred to a copy editor or producer. The producer's rundown is coded to show the status of each item that is being worked on. One BBC editor referred to a producer "going green." The editor meant the producer had received and approved the majority of the broadcast, and so the producer rundown screen was showing mainly "green" flags, meaning the items were ready for air.

The copy editor, a video editor, a producer, and an anchorperson can retrieve the script in preparation for the broadcast. The script will be sent automatically to the prompter, and after the broadcast is concluded, the rundown and script are automatically archived.

One warning about automation: Automation shifts the responsibility for making certain that the proper action is taken away from the technician in the control area to the journalist and producer in the newsroom. Automation systems only do what they are told to do. A typing mistake can set off a disastrous sequence of events. Automation puts the focus of responsibility on the story creator and the program producer.

With ENPS, a journalist working in the radio news area at BBC Bristol has access to the evening national TV news script as a source of information. A producer in Wales can preview the same script to see if the story should be retrieved as a video file for insertion in a local Welsh-language broadcast.

CONCLUSION

The BBC ENPS system was evolutionary, not revolutionary. It created better ways to do what earlier systems offered. It's unique quality was its flexibility to deal with a wide variety of terminals, it's ease of use, and a number of user friendly features that overcame some of the user difficulties experienced with other software.

Producers, writers, anchorpersons, and editors all benefit from the speed with which the newsroom computer system accesses materials and sources. However, today each of the BBC journalists must be more skilled at multi-tasking than their predecessors. They may be called upon to write a story, locate video and mark it for editing, and prepare information for the subtitles (character generator) or the Chromakey. Professional journalists have a great assistant in the newsroom computer system. They also have a strict taskmaster. The system requires them to be more accurate, work faster and be technology literate in order to do their jobs well.

Suggested Readings

Cremer, C., Keirstead, P., & Yoakam, R. (1996). *ENG: Television news.* New York: McGraw-Hill.
Featherly, K. (1998). *Guide to building a newsroom Web site.* Washington, DC: RTNDF.
Grant, A. E., & Meadows, J. H. (Ed.). (2002). *Communication technology update* (8th ed.). Woburn, MA: Focal Press.
Heller, B., Lipinski, A. M., & Pruitt, G. (2000). *Roadmap 2005: National vs regional journalism,* symposium. New York: Pew Center for Civic Journalism.
Keirstead, P., & Keirstead, S-K. (1999). *Automating television news: A generation of change.* Tallahassee, FL: Castle Garden Press.
Kienzle, C. (1998, June 1). CNN has a digital future in mind. *TV Technology, 8.*
Massey, K., & Baran, S. (2001). *Introduction to telecommunications converging technologies.* Mountain View, CA: Mayfield Publishing Co.
Murrie, M.(2001). *Local Web news: Case study of nine local broadcast Internet news operations,* Washington, DC: RTNDF.
Redmond, J., Shook, F., & Lattimore, D. (2001). *The broadcast news process* (6th ed.). Englewood, CO: Morton.
Sullivan, S., Zollman, P., & Thalhimer, M. (1999). *Non-stop news.* Washington, DC: RTNDF.
Thalhimer, M. A. (Ed.). (1996). *News in the next century,* Washington, DC: RTNDF.
Tuggle, C A., Carr, F., & Huffman S. (2001). *Broadcast news handbook.* Boston: McGraw-Hill.
Westin, Av. *Practices for television journalists.* Arlington, VA: The Freedom Forum.
Whittemore, H. (1990). *CNN: The inside story* (p. 29). Boston: Little, Brown.
Wickham, K. (1998). *Perspectives; On line journalism.* Boulder, CO: CourseWise.

Index

A

Agence France Presse (AFP), 71
ARPANET, 130
Associated Press, 19, 69, 71, 73, 144–145
    APTV, 48, 72–73
    ENPS electronic news production system, 19, 163–165
    NewsCenter, 19
Autocue, 19
Avid Technology, 19
    AvidiNews, 19, 59, 154–155
    BASYS, 19, 59, 154, 161
AvStar, 19

B

British Broadcasting Corporation (BBC), 71–72, 160–165

C

Cable News Network (CNN), 24, 79, 81, 131, 143, 153–160
Central Office of Information (COI), 71
Character Generator (CG), 21, 125
Chromakey, 21
Closed-Captioning, 21
Comprompter, 19
    NewsKing, 19
Computer-assisted reporting, 130, 137–139
    archives, 131
    Internet, 132, 136, 140
    world wide web (WWW), 130, 134–136, 141

D

Dalet, 19
    Open Media, 19
DCM Data Center Management, 19
Digital Video Effects (DVE), 22

E

Electronic Newsgathering (ENG), 52, 80
Extel, 71

F

Federal Communications Commission (FCC), 96, 103

G

Grotticelli, M., 131

H

HTV West, 79

M

Microwave *see* Electronic news gathering
Multimedia, 150

167

N

NewsKing *see* Comprompter
NewsMaker, 19
NewStar, 19, 64, 67

O

Organizations
    Asian Journalists' Association (AJA), 142
    Association for Women in Communication, 132
    Broadcasters Training Network, 142
    National Association of Black Journalists (NABJ), 142
    National Association of Hispanic Journalists (NAHJ), 142
    National Lesbian and Gay Journalists' Association, 142
    Radio-Television News Directors Association (RTNDA), xv, 141–142
    Radio-Television News Directors Foundation (RTNDF), 135, 142
    Society of Professional Journalists (SPJ), 135, 141–142
    South Asian Journalists' Association (SAJA), 142
    The Minorities in Broadcasting Training Program, 142

P

ParkerVision (PVTV), 126
Poynter Institute, 141–142
Press Association (PA), 71
Press Trust of India (PTI), 71
Prompter, 21, 84, 125

R

Reuters, 48

S

Satellite news vehicle (SNV), 52–54, 80
Still store, 21

T

TASS, 71
TelePrompTer, *see* prompter

U

United Press International (UPI), 69

V

Virtual Reality, 21

W

Wendland, M., 131
Wickham, K, 130
Wright, R., 130

For Product Safety Concerns and Information please contact our EU
representative GPSR@taylorandfrancis.com
Taylor & Francis Verlag GmbH, Kaufingerstraße 24, 80331 München, Germany

www.ingramcontent.com/pod-product-compliance
Lightning Source LLC
Chambersburg PA
CBHW061836300426
44115CB00013B/2403